The hive of "The bee-hunter" : a repository of sketches, including peculiar American character, scenery, and rural sports

Thomas Bangs Thorpe 1815-1878

The Wild Turkey Hunter. (Frontispiece).

THE HIVE

OF

"THE BEE-HUNTER,"

A Repository of Sketches,

INCLUDING

PECULIAR AMERICAN CHARACTER, SCENERY, AND RURAL SPORTS.

BY T. B. THORPE,

OF LOUISIANA.

AUTHOR OF "TOM OWEN, THE BEE-HUNTER;" "MYSTERIES OF THE BACK-WOODS," ETC. ETC.

ILLUSTRATED BY SKETCHES FROM NATURE.

NEW-YORK:

D. APPLETON AND COMPANY,

346 & 348 BROADWAY.

LONDON: 16 LITTLE BRITAIN.

M.DCCC.LIV.

TO

THE LOVERS OF NATURE,

WHETHER RESIDING IN THE CROWDED CITY, PLEASANT
VILLAGE, OR NATIVE WILD,

This Volume

IS CORDIALLY DEDICATED.

PREFACE.

THE " HIVE OF THE BEE-HUNTER" has one object, which the author would impress upon such readers as may honor him with their attention.

An effort has been made, in the course of these sketches, to give to those personally unacquainted with the scenery of the southwest, some idea of the country, its surface, and vegetation.

In these matters, the author has endeavored to be critically correct, indulging in the honest ambition of giving some information, while depicting the germinating evidences of the great original characters national to these localities.

The southwest, with its primeval and evergreen forests, its unbounded prairies, and its many and continuous rivers, presents contributions of nature, which the pilgrims from every land, for the first time, behold with wonder and awe.

Here, in their vast interior solitudes, far removed from trans-Atlantic influences, are alone to be found, in the more comparative infancy of our country, characters truly *sui generis*—truly American.

What man would be, uninfluenced by contact with the varied associations of long civilization, is here partially demonstrated in the denizens of the interior of a mighty continent.

The discovery of America,—its vast extent,—and its developing destiny,—present facts, which far surpass the wildest imagery of the dreamers of the olden times.

There are growing up, in these primitive wilds, men, whose daily life and conversation, when detailed, form exaggerations; but whose histories are, after all, only the natural developments of the mighty associations which surround them.

CONTENTS.

8 CONTENTS.

WILD TURKEY HUNTING.

ORIGINALLY, the wild turkey was found scattered throughout the whole of our continent, its habits only differing, where the peculiarity of the seasons compelled it to provide against excessive cold or heat. In the "clearing," it only lives in its excellent and degenerated descendant of the farm-yard, but in the vast prairies and forests of the "far west," this bird is still abundant, and makes an important addition to the fare of wild life.

It is comparatively common on the "frontiers," but every passing year lessens its numbers; and as their disappearance always denotes their death, their extermination is progressive and certain.

In Louisiana, Alabama, South Carolina, and other southern states, there are fastnesses, in which they will find support and protection for a long time to come. The swamps and lowlands that offer no present inducement to " the settler," will shelter them from the rifle ; and in the rich productions of the soil, they find a super-abundance of food.

The same obscurity, however, that protects them, leaves the hole of the wildcat in peace ; and this bitter enemy of the turkey, wars upon it, and makes its life one of cunning and care. Nor, is its finely-flavored meat unappreciated by other destroyers, as the fox often makes the turkey an evening meal, while the weasel contents itself with the little chicks. The nest, however, may have been made, and the young birds may have in peace broken the shell, and frightened at their own piping notes, hidden instinctively away, when the Mississippi will rise, bearing upon its surface the waters of a thousand floods, swell within its narrow banks, and overflow the lowlands. The young bird, unable to fly, and too delicate to resist the influence of the wet, sickens and dies.

Upon the *dryness* of the season, therefore, the turkey-hunter builds his hopes of the plentifulness of the game.

Independent of the pernicious influence of unfavorable seasons, or the devastation of the wild turkey by destructive animals, their numbers are also annually lessened by the skill of the pioneer and backwoodsman, and in but comparatively a few more years the bird must have, as a denizen of our border settlements, only a traditionary existence ; for the turkey is not migratory in its habits, and its absence from any of its accustomed haunts, is indicative of its total extermination from the place where it was once familiar.

At present, the traveller in the " far west," while wending his solitary way through the trackless forests, sometimes very unexpectedly meets a drove of turkeys in his pathway, and when his imagination suddenly warms with the thought that he is near the poultry-yard of some hospitable farmer, and while his wearied limbs seem to labor with extra pain, as he thinks of the couch compared with the cold ground as a resting-place, he hears a sudden whizzing in the air, a confused noise, and his seeming evidences of civilization and comfort vanish as the wild turkey disappears, giving him by their precipitate flight, the most painful evidence that he is far from the haunts of men and home.

Turkey hunting is a favorite pursuit with all who can practise it with success, but it is a bird liberally provided by nature with the instinct of self-preservation, and is, therefore, seldom found off its guard. Skilful indeed must be the shot that stops the turkey in its flight of alarm, and yet its wings, as with the partridge and quail, are little used for the purposes of escaping from danger. It is on their speed that they rely for safety, and we doubt if the best hounds could catch them in a race, even if the turkey's wings were clipped so that they could not resort to height to elude their pursuers. So little indeed does the bird depend upon its pinions, that they find it difficult to cross rivers moderately wide, and in the attempt the weak and very fat, are often sacrificed.

We have seen the wild turkey gathering in troops upon the limb of some tall cotton wood on the banks of the Mississippi, and we have known by their preparations that they intended to cross the river. There on their elevated roost they would set, stretching out their necks as if gathering a long breath for their, to them, prolonged flight. In the mean while, the "squatter," on the opposite bank, would prepare himself to take advantage of the birds' necessities. Judging from experience where about the "drove" would land on his side of the stream, he would lie concealed until the flight commenced. The birds would finally launch themselves in the mid air, as in their progress it could be seen that they constantly descended toward the earth,—the bank would be reached, but numbers exhausted would fail to reach the land, and would fall a prey to the insatiate wave, or the rapacious wants of man.

In hunting the wild turkey, there is unfortunately too little excitement to make it a favorite sport with those who follow the hounds. But the uncertainty of meeting with the bird, even if you know its haunts, and the sudden termination of the sport, even if successful, makes successful turkey hunters few and far between.

The cautiousness of the wild turkey is extraordinary: it excels that of the deer, or any other game whatever;

and nothing but stratagem, and an intimate knowledge of the habits of the bird by the hunter, will command success. We once knew an Indian, celebrated for all wood craft, who made a comfortable living by supplying a frontier town with game. Often did he greet the villagers with loads of venison, with grouse, with bear, but seldom, indeed, did he offer the esteemed turkey for sale. Upon being reproached for his seeming incapacity to kill the turkey, by those who desired the bird, he defended himself as follows:

"Me meet moose—he stop to eat, me shoot him. Me meet bear—he climb a tree, no see Indian, me shoot him. Me meet deer—he look up—say may be Indian, may be stump—and me shoot him. Me see turkey great way off—he look up and say, Indian coming sure—me no shoot turkey, he cunning too much."

The turkey is also very tenacious of life, and will often escape though wounded in a manner that would seem to defy the power of locomotion. A rifle ball has been driven through and through the body of a turkey, and yet it has run with speed for miles. Some hunters have been fortunate in possessing dogs that have, without any instruction, been good turkey hunters. These dogs follow the scent, lead the hunter up to the haunts of the bird, lie quiet until a shot is had, and then follow the game if only wounded, until it is exhausted, and thus secure a prize to the hunter, that would otherwise have been lost. This manner of hunting the turkey, however, cannot be called its most legitimate form; as will be noticed in the progress of our chronicle.

The taste that makes the deer and fox hunt a favorite amusement, is not the foundation on which to build a true turkey hunter. The baying of hounds, the clamor of the horn, the excitement of the chase, the pell-mell and noisy demonstration, are all destructive to the successful pursuit of the turkey,—consequently, the turkey hunter is distinct and peculiar; he sympathises with the excentric habits of the bird, with its love of silence, with its obscurity, and it is no objection to him, if the morning is whiled away in the deep solitude, in comparative inaction, for all this favors contemplation worthy of an intellectual mind.

It is unnecessary to describe the bird, though we never see it fairly represented except in the forest. The high-mettled racer that appears upon the course is no more superior to the well fed cart-horse, than is the wild turkey to the tame; in fact, nothing living shows more points of health and purity of blood than this noble bird. Its game head, and clear hazel eye, the clean, firm step, the great breadth of shoulder, and deep chest, strike the most superficial observer. Then there is an absolute commanding beauty about them, when they are alarmed or curious; then they elevate themselves to their full height, bringing their head perpendicular with their feet, and gaze about, every feather in its place, the foot upraised ready at an instant to strike off at a speed, that, as has been said of the ostrich, " scorneth the horse and his rider."

As a general thing, turkey-hunters, if they be of literary habits, read Isaak Walton, and Burton's " Anatomy of Melancholy," and all—learned or unlearned—are, of course, enthusiastic disciples of the rod and line. The piscator can be an enthusiastic admirer of the opera, the wild turkey-hunter could not be, for his taste never carries him beyond the simple range of natural notes. Herein, he excels.

Place him in the forest with his pipe, and no rough Pan ever piped more wilily, or more in harmony with the scenes around him. The same tube modulates the sound of alarm, and the dulcet strains of love; it plays plaintively the complaining notes of the female, and, in sweet chirrups, calls forth the lover from his hiding-place; it carols among the low whisperings of the fledgling, and expresses the mimic sounds of joy at the treasure of food, that is discovered under the fallen leaf, or half hidden away in the decaying wood.

And all this is done so craftily, that ears, on which nature has set her stamp of peculiar delicacy, and the instinct, true almost as the shadow to the sunlight; are both deceived.

The wild turkey-hunter is a being of solitude. There is no noise or boisterous mirth in his pursuit.

Even the dead leaf, as it sails in circuitous motion to the earth, intrudes upon his caution, and alarms the wary game, which, in its care of preservation, flies as swiftly before the imaginary, as before the real danger.

Often, indeed, is the morning's work destroyed by the cracking of a decayed limb, under the nimble spring of the squirrel. The deer and timid antelope will stop to gratify curiosity; the hare scents the air for an instant, when alarmed, before it dashes off; but the turkey never speculates, never wonders; suspicion of danger, prompts it to immediate flight, as quickly as a reality.

The implements of the turkey-hunter are few and simple; the "call," generally made of the large bone of the turkey's wing, or a small piece of wood, into which is driven a nail, and a small piece of oil stone (the head of the nail on being quickly scraped on the stone, producing perfectly the noise of the female turkey), and a double-barrel fowling-piece, complete the list. A rifle is used where the game is plentiful; and the person using it, as we have already described, depends upon the sagacity and speed of the dog, to rescue the wounded bird, for the turkey never instantly dies, except wounded in the brain.

Where turkeys are plentiful and but little hunted, unskilful persons succeed in killing them; of such hunters we shall not speak.

The bird changes its habits somewhat with its haunts, growing wilder as it is most pursued; it may, therefore, be said to be the wildest of game. Gaining in wisdom according to the necessity, it is a different bird where it is constantly sought for as game, from where it securely lives in the untrodden solitude. The turkey will, therefore, succeed at times in finding a home in places comparatively "thickly settled," and be so seldom seen, that they are generally supposed to be extinct. Under such circumstances, they fall victims only to the very few hunters who may be said to make a science of their pursuit.

"I rather think," said a turkey-hunter, " if you want to find a thing *very cunning*, you need not go to the fox or such varmints, but take a gobbler. I once hunted regular after the same one for three years, and never saw him twice.

"I knew the critter's 'yelp' as well as I know Music's, my old deer dog ; and his track was as plain to me as the trail of a log hauled through a dusty road.

"I hunted the gobbler always in the same 'range,' and about the same 'scratchins,' and he got so, at last, that when I 'called,' he would run from me, *taking the opposite direction to my own foot-tracks*.

"Now, the old rascal kept a great deal on a ridge, at the end of which, where it lost itself in the swamp, was a hollow cypress tree. Determined to outwit him, I put on my shoes, *heels foremost*, walked leisurely down the ridge, and got into the hollow tree, and gave a 'call,' and boys," said the speaker exultingly, " it would have done you good to see that turkey coming towards me on a trot, looking at my tracks, and thinking I had *gone the other way*."

Of all turkey-hunters, our friend W—— is the most experienced ; he is a bachelor, lives upon his own plantation, studies, philosophizes, makes fishing tackle, and kills turkeys. With him, it is a science reduced to certainty. Place him in the woods where turkeys frequent, and he is as certain of them as if already in his possession.

He understands the habits of the bird so well, that he will, on his first essay, on a new hunting-ground, give the exact character of the hunters the turkeys have been accustomed to deal with. The most crafty turkeys are those which W—— seeks, hemmed in by plantations, inhabiting uncultivatable land, and always in more or less danger of pursuit and discovery, they become, under such circumstances, wild beyond any game whatever.

They seem incapable of being deceived, and taking every thing strange, as possessed to them of danger— whether it be a moth out of season—or a veteran hunter—they appear to common, or even uncommon observers, annihilated from the country, were it not for their footprints occasionally to be seen in the soft soil beside the running stream, or in the light dust in the beaten road.

A veteran gobbler, used to all the tricks of the hunter's art—one who has had his wattles cut with shot; against whose well-defended breast had struck the spent ball of the rifle—one who, though almost starved, would walk by the treasures of grain in the " trap" and

o will listen to the plaintive note of
s tried its quavers, its length, its re-
e nature has given him—and then,
except in a smothered voice, for
;—such a turkey will W—— se-
with, and, in spite of the chances

re the best specimen of wild tur-
ition of skill between the perfec-
nct, and the superior intellect

, armed with his " call," starts
into the forest; he bears upon his shoulder the trusty
gun. He is either informed of the presence of turkeys,
and has a particular place or bird in view, or he makes
his way cautiously along the banks of some running
steam; his progress is slow and silent; it may be that
he unexpectedly hears a noise, sounding like distant
thunder; he then knows that he is in close proximity
of the game, and that he has disturbed it to flight.
When such is the case, his work is comparatively done.

We will, for illustration, select a more difficult hunt.
The day wears towards noon, the patient hunter has
met no " sign," when suddenly a slight noise is heard—
not unlike, to unpractised ears, a thousand other wood-
land sounds; the hunter listens; again the sound is
heard, as if a pebble dropped into the bosom of a little
lake. It may be that woodpecker, who, desisting from

his labors, has opened his bill to yawn—or, perchance, yonder little bird so industriously scratching among the dead leaves of that young holly. Again, precisely the same sound is heard; yonder, high in the heavens, is a solitary hawk, winging its way over the forests, its rude scream etherealized, might come down to our ears, in just such a sound as made the turkey-hunter listen; —again the same note—now more distinct. The quick ear of the hunter is satisfied; stealthily he intrenches himself behind a fallen tree, a few green twigs are placed before him, from among which protrudes the muzzle of his deadly weapon.

Thus prepared, he takes his "call," and gives one solitary "*cluck*"—so exquisitely—that it chimes in with the running brook and the rustling leaf.

It may be, that a half a mile off, if the place be favorable for conveying sound, is feeding a "gobbler;" prompted by his nature, as he quickly scratches up the herbage that conceals his food, he gives utterance to the sounds that first attracted the hunter's attention.

Poor bird! he is bent on filling his crop; his feelings are listless, common-place; his wings are awry; the plumage on his breast seems soiled with rain; his wattles are contracted and pale,—look! he starts— every feather is instantly in its place, he raises his delicate game-looking head full four feet from the ground, and listens; what an eye! what a stride is suggested by that lifted foot! gradually the head sinks; again the bright plumage grows dim, and with a low *cluck*, he resumes his search for food.

The treasures of the American forest are before him; the choice pecan-nut is neglected for that immense "grub worm" that rolls down the decayed stump, too large to crawl; now that grasshopper is nabbed; presently a hill of ants presents itself, and the bird leans over it, and, with wondering curiosity, peering down the tiny hole of its entrance, out of which are issuing the industrious insects.

Again that *cluck* greets his ear, up rises the head with lightning swiftness, the bird starts forward a pace or two, looks around in wonder, and answers back.

No sound is heard but the falling acorn; and it fairly echoes, as it rattles from limb to limb, and dashes off to the ground.

The bird is uneasy—he picks pettishly, smooths down his feathers, elevates his head slowly, and then brings it to the earth; raises his wings as if for flight, jumps upon the limb of a fallen tree, looks about, settles down finally into a brown study, and evidently commences thinking.

An hour may have elapsed—he has resolved the matter over; his imagination has become inflamed; he has heard just enough to *wish to hear more;* he is satisfied, that no turkey-hunter uttered the sounds that reached his ear, for they were *too few and far between;* and then there rises up in his mind some disconsolate mistress, and he gallantly flies down from his low perch, gives his body a swaggering motion, and utters a distinct and prolonged *cluck*—significant of both surprise and joy.

On the instant, the dead twigs near by crack beneath a heavy tread, and he starts off under the impression that he is caught; but the meanderings of some ruminating cow inform him of his mistake. Composing himself, he listens—ten minutes since he challenged, when a low cluck in the distance reaches his ears.

Now, our gobbler is an old bird, and has several times, as if by a miracle, escaped from harm with his life; he has grown very cunning indeed.

He will not roost two successive nights upon the same tree, so that daylight never exposes him to the hunter, who has hidden himself away in the night to kill him in the morning's dawn.

He never gobbles without running a short distance at least, as if alarmed at the noise he makes himself—he presumes every thing is suspicious and dangerous, and his experience has heightened the instinct.

Twice, when young, was he coaxed within gun-shot: but got clear by some fault of the percussion-caps—after that, he was fooled by an idle schoolboy, who was a kind of ventriloquist, and would have been slain, had not the urchin overloaded his gun.

Three times did he come near being killed by heedlessly wandering with his thoughtless playfellows.

Once he was caught in a "pen," and got out by an overlooked hole in its top.

Three feathers of last year's "fan," decayed under the weight of a spring-trap.

All this experience has made him a "deep" bird; and he will sit and plume himself, when common hunters are tooting away, but never so wisely as to deceive him twice. They all reveal themselves by overstepping the modesty of nature, and *woo him too much;* his loves are far more coy, far less intrusive.

Poor bird! he does not know that W—— is spreading his snare for him, and is even then so sure of his victim, as to be revolving in his mind whether his goodly carcass should be a present to a newly-married friend, or be served up in savory fumes, from his own bachelor but hospitable board.

The last *cluck* heard by the gobbler, fairly roused him, and he presses forward; at one time he runs with speed; then stops as if not yet quite satisfied; something turns him back; still he lingers only for a moment in his course, until coming to a running stream, where he will have to fly; the exertion seems too much for him.

Stately parading in the full sunshine, he walks along the margin of the clear water, admiring his fine person as it is reflected in the sylvan mirror, and then, like some vain lover, tosses his head, as if to say, "let them come to me:" the listless gait is resumed, expressive that the chase is given up.

Gaining the ascent of a low bank, that lines the stream he has just deserted, he stops at the foot of a young beech; in the green moss that fills the interstices of the otherwise smooth bark is hidden away a cricket; the turkey picks at it, without catching it; something annoys him.

Like the slipper of Cinderella to the imagination of the young prince, or the glimpses of a waving ringlet or jewelled hand, to the glowing passions of a young heart, is the remembrance of that sound, that now full two hours since was first heard by our hero—and has been, in that long time, but *twice* repeated. He speculates that in the shady woods that surround him, there must wander a mate; solitarily she plucks her food, and calls for me—the monster man, impatient of his prey, doles not out his music so softly or so daintily—I am not deceived, and, by my ungallant fears, she will be won by another.

Cluck.—

How well-timed the call. The gobbler now entirely off his guard, contracts himself, opens wide his mouth, and rolls forth, fearlessly, a volume of sound for his answer.

The stream is crossed in a flutter, the toes scarce indent themselves in the soft ground over which they pass. On, on he plunges, until caution again brings him to a halt. We could almost wish that so fine a bird might escape—that there might be given one "call" too much—one, that grated unnaturally on the poor bird's ear—but not so,—they lead him to his doom, filling his heart with hope and love.

To the bird there is one strange incongruity in the "call"—never before has he gone so far with so little success; but the note is perfect, the time most nicely given.

Again he rolls forth a loud response, and listens—yet no answer: his progress is still slow.

The *cluck* again greets his ear; there was a slight quaver attached to it this time, like the forming of a second note; he is nearing his object of pursuit, and with an energetic "call;" he rushes forward, his long neck stretched out, and his head moving inquiringly from side to side.

No longer going round the various obstacles he meets with in his path, but impatiently flying over them, he comes to an open space, and stops.

Some six hundred yards from where he stands may be seen a fallen tree; you can observe some green brush, that looks as if it grew out of the very decayed wood; in this "brush" is hidden away the deadly fowling piece, and its muzzle is protruding towards the open ground. Behind it is the hunter, flat upon the ground, yet so placed that the weapon is at his shoulder. He seems to be as dead as the tree in front of him. Could you watch him closely, you would perceive that he scarcely winks for fear of alarming his game.

2

The turkey, still in his exposed situation, gobbles :—on the instant the hunter raises his "call" to his lips, and gives a prolonged *cluck*—loud and shrill; the first that could really be construed by the turkey into a direct answer.

The noble bird, now certain of success, fairly dances with delight; he starts forward, his feathers and neck amorously playing as he advances; now he commences his "strut"—his slender body swells, the beautiful plumage of his breast unfolds itself—his neck curves, drawing the neck downward—the wattles grow scarlet, while the skin that covers the head changes like rainbow tints. The long feathers of the wings brush the ground, the tail rises and opens into a semicircle, the gorgeously colored head becomes beautifully relieved in its centre.

On he comes, with a hitching gait, glowing in the sunshine with purple and gold.

The siren *cluck* is twice repeated; he contracts his form to the smallest dimensions; upwards rises the head to the highest point; he stands upon his very toes, and looks suspiciously around; fifty yards of distance protects him from the bolt of death: he even condescends to pick about.

What a trial for the expectant hunter! how vividly does he recollect that one breath too much has spoiled a morning's work!

The minutes wear on, and the bird again becomes the *caller*; he gobbles, opens his form, and, when fully bloomed out, the enchanting *cluck* greets his ear; on, on he comes—like the gay horse towards the inspiring music of the drum, or like a bark beating against the wind, gallantly but slowly.

The dark cold barrel of the gun is now not more silent than is the hunter; the game is playing just outside the very edge of its deadly reach; the least mistake, and it is gone.

One gentle zephyr, one falling twig, might break the charm, and make nature revolt at the coyness apparent in the mistress, and then the lover would wing his way full of life to the woods.

But on he comes—so still is every thing that you hear his wings distinctly as they brush the ground, while the sun plays in conflicting rays and colored lights about his gaudily bronzed plumage.

Suddenly, the woods ring in echoing circles back upon you; a sharp report is heard.

Out starts, alarmed by the noise, a blue jay, which squalls as he passes in waving lines before you, so rudely wakened was he from sleep.

But our rare and beautiful bird,—our gallant and noble bird,—our cunning and game bird, where is he?

The glittering plumage—the gay step—the bright eye—all—all are gone:—

Without a movement of the muscles, our valorous lover has fallen lifeless to the earth.

SUMMER RETREAT IN ARKANSAS.

IT is not expected that a faithful description of Satan's Summer Retreat in Arkansas, will turn aside the fashion of two worlds, from Brighton and Bath, or from Newport and Saratoga, although the residents in the neighborhood of that delightful place, profess to have ocular demonstration, as well as popular opinion, that his Satanic Majesty in warm weather regularly retires to the " Retreat," and " there reclines " in the " cool."

The solemn grandeur that surrounds this distinguished resort, is worthy of the hero as represented by Milton; its characteristics are darkness, gloom and mystery; it is environed by the unrivalled vegetation and forest of the Mississippi valley. View it when you will, whether decked out in all the luxuriance of a southern summer, or stripped of its foliage by the winter's blasts—it matters not—its grandeur is always sombre.

The huge trees seem immortal, their roots look as if they struck to the centre of the earth, while the gnarled limbs reach out to the clouds   Here and there may be seen one of these lordly specimens of vegetation, furrowed by the lightning; from its top to the base you can trace the subtle fluid in its descent, and see where it shattered off the gigantic limb, or turned aside from slight inequality in the bark.

These stricken trees, no longer able to repel the numerous parasites that surround them, soon become festooned with wreathes and flowers; while the damp air engenders on living tree and dead, like funereal drapery, the pendant moss, which waves in every breeze and seems to cover the whole scene with the gloom of the grave.

Rising out of this forest, for ten square miles, is the dense cane-brake, that bears the name of " Satan's Summer Retreat;" it is formed by a space of ground where, seemingly, from its superiority of soil, more delicate vegetation than that which surrounds it, has usurped the empire.   Here the reed, which the disciple of Izaak Walton plays over the northern streams like a wand, grows into a delicate mast—springing with the prodigality of grass from the rich alluvium that gives it sustenance, and tapering from its roots to the height of twenty or thirty feet, it there mingles in compact and luxuriant confusion its long leaves.

A portion of this brake is interwoven with vines of all descriptions, which makes it so thick that it is al-

most as impenetrable as a mountain. Here, in this solitude, where the noon-day sun never penetrates, myriads
of birds, with the instinct of safety, roost at night;
and at the dawn of day for awhile darken the air as
they seek their haunts—their manure deadening like a
a fire, for acres around, the vegetation, so long have they
possessed the solitude.

Amid this mass of cane and vine, the black bear
retire for winter quarters, where they pass the season,
if not disturbed, in the insensibility of sleep, and yet
come out in the spring as fat as when they commenced
their long nap.

The forest, the waste, and the dangers of the cane-
brake, but add to the excitement of the Arkansas hunter;
he conquers them all, and makes them subservient to
his pursuits. Familiar with these scenes, they to him
possess no sentiment; he builds his log cabin in a clearing made by his own hands, amid the surrounding grandeur, and it looks like a gypsy hut among the ruins of
a Gothic cathedral. The noblest trees to him are only
valuable for fence-rails; and the cane-brake is "an infernal dark hole," where you can "see sights," "catch
bear," and get a "fish pole," ranging in size from a
"penny whistle to that of a young stove pipe."

The undoubted hero of Satan's Summer Retreat, is
old Bob Herring: he has a character that would puzzle
three hundred metaphysicians consecutively. For, while
he is as bold as a lion, he is superstitious as an Indian.

The exact place of his birth he cannot tell, as he says that his parents " travelled " as long as he can remember them. He " squatted " on the Mississippi at its nearest point to the Retreat, and there erecting a rude camp, commenced hunting for a living, having no prospect ahead but selling out his " pre-emption right " and improvements, and again squatting somewhere else.

Unfortunately, the extent of Arkansas, and the swamp that surrounded Bob's location, kept it out of market until, to use his own language, he " became the ancientest inhabitant in the hull of Arkansaw." And having, in spite of himself, gradually formed acquaintances with the few residents in this vicinity, and grown into importance from his knowledge of the country, and his hunting exploits, he has established himself for life, at what he calls, the " Wasp's diggins ;" made a potato patch, which he has never had time to fence in ; talked largely of a cornfield ; and hung his cabin round with rifle-pouches, gourds, red peppers, and flaming advertisements with rampant horses and pedigrees ; these latter ornaments, he looks upon as rather sentimental—but he excuses himself on the ground that they look " hoss," and he considers such an expression as considerably characteristic of himself.

We have stated that Bob's mind would puzzle three hundred metaphysicians consecutively, and we as boldly assert that an equal number of physiologists would be brought to a stand by his personal appearance. The

left side of his face is good looking, but the right side
seems to be under the influence of an invisible air-pump;
it looks drawn out of shape; his perpendicular height
is six feet one inch, but that gives the same idea of his
length that the diameter gives of the circumference;
how long Bob Herring would be if he were drawn
out, it is impossible to tell. Bob himself says, that he
was made on too tall a scale for this world, and that he
was shoved in like the joints of a telescope,—poor in
flesh, his enormous bones and joints rattle when he
moves, and they would no doubt long since have fallen
apart, but for the enormous tendons that bind them together as visibly as a good sized hawser would.

Such is Bob Herring,—who on a bear hunt will do
more hard work, crack more jokes, and be more active
than any man living; sustaining the whole with unflinch-
ing good humor, never getting angry except when he
breaks his whiskey-bottle, or has a favorite dog open on
the wrong trail.

My first visit to Satan's Summer Retreat, was pro-
pitious; my companions were all choice spirits; the
weather was fine, and Bob Herring inimitable. The
bustling scene that prefaced the "striking the camp"
for night lodgings, was picturesque and animated; a
long ride brought us to our halting-place, and there was
great relief in again stepping on the ground.

Having hoppled our horses, we next proceeded to
build a fire, which was facilitated by taking advantage

Bob Herring's Camp-fire.

of a dead tree for a back-log; our saddles, guns, and other necessaries were brought within the circle of its light, and lolling upon the ground we partook of a frugal supper, the better to be prepared for our morrow's exertions and our anticipated breakfast.

Beds were next made up, and few can be better than a good supply of cane tops, covered with a blanket, with a saddle for a pillow; upon such a rude couch, the hunter sleeps more soundly than the effeminate citizen on his down. The crescent moon with her attendant stars, studded the canopy under which we slept, and the blazing fire completely destroyed the chilliness of a southern December night.

The old adage of "early to bed and early to rise" was intended to be acted upon, that we might salute the tardy sun with the heat of our sport; and probably we would have carried out our intentions, had not Bob Herring very coolly asked if any of us snored "unkimmonly loud," for he said his *old shooting iron* would go off at a good imitation of a bear's breathing. This sally from Bob brought us all upright, and then there commenced a series of jibes, jokes, and stories, that no one can hear or witness except on an Arkansas hunt with "old coons." Bob, like the immortal Jack, was witty himself, and the cause of wit in others; but he sustained himself against all competition, and gave in his notions and experience with an unrivalled humor and simplicity.

He found in me an attentive listener, and, therefore, went into details, until he talked every one but myself asleep.

From general remarks, he changed to addressing me personally, and as I had every thing to learn, he went from the elementary, to the most complex experience.

" You are green in bar hunting," said he to me, in a commiserating tone—" green as a jimson weed—but don't get short-winded 'bout it, case it's a thing like readin', to be l'arnt ;—a man don't come it perfectly at once, like a dog does ; and as for that, *they* l'arn a heap in time ;—thar is a greater difference 'tween a pup and an old dog on a bar hunt, than thar is 'tween a militia man and a regler. I remember when *I could'nt bar hunt*, though the thing seems onpossible now ; it only takes time—a true eye and a steady hand, though I did know a fellow that called himself a doctor, who said you could'nt do it, if you was narvious.

" I asked him if he meant by that, agee and fever !

" He said, it was the agee without the fever.

" Thar *may* be such a thing as narvious, stranger, but nothing but a yarth quake, or the agee can shake me ; and still bar hunting aint as easy as scearing a wild turkey, by a long shot.

" The varmint aint a hog, to run with a— w—h—e—w ; just corner one—cotch its cub, or cripple it, and if you don't have to fight, or get out of the way, then thar aint no cat-fish in the Mississip. I larnt that nih twenty year ago, and, perhaps, you would like to know about it." Signifying my assent, Bob Herring got up on his bed—for as it was upon the bare ground, he could not well get off of it,—and, approaching the fire, he threw about a cord of wood upon it, in the form of a few huge logs; as they struck the blazing heap, the sparks flew upwards in the clear cold air, like jets of stars; then, fixing himself most comfortably, he detailed what follows :

" I had a knowin old sow on a time, that would have made a better hunter than any dog ever heer'd on— she had such a nose,—talk 'bout a *dog* following a cold trail—she'd track a bar through running water. Well —you see afor' I know'd her vartu', she came running into my cabin, bristles up, and fell on the floor, from what I now believe, to have been a regular scear. I thought she'd seen a bar, for nothing else could make her run ; and, taking down my rifle, I went out sort a carelessly, with only two dogs at my heels. I hadn't gone far 'fore I saw a bar, sure enough, quietly standing beside a small branch—it was an old *He*, and no mistake.

" I crawled up to him on my hands and knees, and raised my rifle, but had I fired, I must have hit him so far in front, that the ball would have ranged back and not cut his mortals. I waited—and he turned tail towards me, and started across the branch ; afeer'd I'd lose him, I blazed away, and a sort of cut him slantingdicularly through his hams, and brought him down; thar he sot looking like a sick nigger with the dropsy, or a black bale of cotton turned up on end. It was not a judge-matical shot, and Smith thar," pointing at one of the sleeping hunters, "would say so."

Hereupon Bob Herring, without any ceremony, seized a long stick, and thrust it into Smith's short ribs, who thus suddenly awakened from a sound sleep, seized his knife, and, looking about him, asked confusedly what was the matter?

"Would you," inquired Bob, very leisurely, "would you—under any carcumstances, shoot an old He in the hams?"

Smith, very peremptorily, told his questioner to go where the occupier of the Retreat in summer, is supposed to reside through the winter months, and went instantly to sleep again.

Bob continued—"Stranger, the bar—as I have said, was on his hams, and thar he sot—waiting to whip somebody, and not knowing where to begin; when the two dogs that followed me came up, and pitched into him like a caving bank—I know'd the result afore the fight began; Blucher had his whole scalp, ears and all, hanging over his nose in a minute, and Tige', was lying some distance from the bar on his back, breathing like a horse with the thumps; he wiped them both out with one stroke of his left paw, and thar he sot—knowing as well as I did, that he was not obliged to the dogs for

the hole in his carcass—and thar I stood like a fool—
rifle in hand, watching him, instead of giving him another ball.   All of a sudden he caught a glimpse of my
hunting shirt, and the way that he walked at me on his
two fore legs, was a caution to slow dogs.

"I fired, and instantly stept round behind the trunk
of a large tree; my second shot confused the bar, and
as he was hunting about for me, just as I was patch-
ing my ball, he again saw me, and, with his ears nailed
back to his head, he gave the d——t w—h—e—w I ever
heard, and made straight at me; I leapt up a bank near
by, and as I gained the top, my foot touched the eend
of his nose.

"If I ever had the '*narvious*,' stranger, that was
the time, for the skin of my face seemed an inch thick,
and my eyes had more rings in them than a wild cat's.

"At this moment, several of my dogs, that war out
on an expedition of their own, came up, and immediately
made battle with the bar, who shook off the dogs in a
flash, and made agin at me; the thing was done so
quick, that as I raised my rifle, I stepped back and fell
over, and, thinking my time was come, wished that I
had been born to be hung, and not chaw'd up; but the
bar didn't cotch me; his hind quarters, as he came at
me, fell into a hole about a root, and caught: I was on
my feet, and out of his reach in a wink, but as quick as
I did this, he had cut through a green root the size of
my leg, he did it in about two snaps, but, weakened by

the exertion, the dogs got hold of him, and held on while I blowed his heart out. Ever since that time, I have been wide awake with a wounded bar—*sartainty or stand off*, being my motto.

"I shall dream of that bar to-night," concluded Bob, fixing his blanket over him; and a few moments only elapsed before he was in danger of his life, if his rifle would go off, as he had said, at a good imitation of a bear's breathing.

Fortunately for me, the sun on the following morn was fairly above the horizon before our little party was ready for the start. While breakfast was being prepared, the rifles were minutely examined; some were taken apart, and every precaution used to insure a quick and certain fire. A rude breakfast having been despatched, lots were drawn who should go into the *drive* with the dogs, as this task in Satan's Summer Retreat is any thing but a pleasant one, being obliged often to walk on the bending cane, which is so thick for hundreds of yards that you cannot touch or see the ground, —then crawling on your hands and knees between roots, you are sometimes brought to a complete halt, and obliged to cut your way through with the knife. While this is going on, the hunters are at *the stands*, places which their judgments dictate as most likely to be passed by the bear when roused by the dogs.

Two miles might, on this occasion, have been passed over by those in the drive in the course of three hours, and yet, although signs were plenty as "leaves," not a bear was started. Hard swearing was heard, and as the vines encircled the feet, or caught one under the nose, it was increased.

In the midst of this ill humor, a solitary bark was heard,—some one exclaimed, that was Bose!—another shrill yelp—that sounded like Music's;—breathing was almost suspended in the excitement of the moment,— presently another and another bark was heard in quick succession—in a minute more *the whole pack of thirty- five stanch dogs* opened!

The change from silence to so much noise, made it almost deafening. Nothing but personal demonstration could give an idea of the effect upon the mind of such a pack baying a bear in a cane-brake. Before me were old hunters; they had been moving along as if destitute of energy or feeling; but now, their eyes flashed, their lips were compressed, and their cheeks flushed; they seemed incapable of fatigue. As for myself, my feelings almost overcame me. I felt a cold sweat stealing down my back, my breath was thick and hot, and as I sus- pended it, to hear more distinctly the fight,—for by this time the dogs had evidently come up with the bear—I could hear the pulsation of my heart.

One minute more to listen—to learn in which direc- tion the war was raging—and then our party unanimously sent forth a yell that would have frightened a nation of Indians

The bear was in his bed when the dogs first came up with him, and did not leave it until the pack surrounded him ; then finding things rather too warm, he broke off with a " whew " that was awful to hear.

His course was towards us on the left, and as he went by, the cane cracked and smashed as if rode over by an insane locomotive. Bob Herring gave the dogs a salute as they passed close at the beast's heels, and the noise increased, until he said, " it sounded as if all *h–ll* were pounding bark."

The bear was commented on as he rushed by; one said he was a " buster ;" " a regular-built eight year old " said another; " fat as a candle," shouted a third; —" he's the beauty of Satan's Summer Retreat, with a band of music after him," sang Bob Herring.

Out of his lair the bear plunged so swiftly, that our greatest exertions scarcely enabled us to keep within hearing distance; his course carried him towards those at the stands, he turned and exactly retraced his course, but not with the same speed; want of breath had several times brought him to a stand, and a fight with the dogs. He passed us the second time within two hundred yards, and coming against a fallen tree, backed up against it, showing a determination, if necessary, there to die.

We made our way towards the spot as fast as the obstacles in our way would let us; the hunters anxious to dispatch him, that few dogs as possible might be sacrificed. The few minutes necessary to accomplish this, seemed *an age*—the fight all the time sounding terrible, for every now and then the bear evidently made a rush at the dogs as they narrowed their circle, or came individually, too near his person.

Crawling through and over the cane-brake, was a new thing to me, and in the prevailing excitement my feet seemed tied together, and there was always a vine directly under my chin to cripple my exertions. While thus struggling, I heard a suspicious cracking in my ear, and looking round, I saw Bob Herring a foot taller than usual, stalking over the cane like a colossus; he very much facilitated my progress by a shove in the rear.

"Come along, stranger," he shouted, his voice as clear as a bell, "come along; the bar and the dogs are going it like a high-pressure political meeting, and I must be thar to put in a word, sartain."

Fortunately for my wind, I was nearer the contest than I imagined, for Bob Herring stopped just ahead of me, examined his rifle, with two or three other hunters just arrived from the stands, and by peeping through the undergrowth, we discovered within thirty yards of us, the fierce raging fight.

Nothing distinctly, however, was seen; a confused mass of legs, heads, and backs of dogs, flying about as if attached to a ball, was all we could make out. On still nearer approach, confusion would clear off for a moment, and the head of the bear could be seen, his

tongue covered with dust and hanging a foot from his
mouth; his jaws covered with foam and blood, and his
eyes almost protruding from their sockets, while his
ears were so closely pressed to the back of his head,
that he seemed destitute of those appendages; the whole,
indicative of unbounded rage and terror. These
glimpses of the bear were only momentary, his perse-
cutors rested but for a breath, and then closed in, regardless of their own lives; for you could discover, mingled with the sharp bark of defiance, the yell that told
of death.

It was only while the bear was crushing some luckless
dog, that they could cover his back, and lacerate it with
their teeth. Bob Herring, and one of the hunters, in
spite of the danger, crept upon their knees, so near,
that it seemed as if another foot advanced would bring
them within the circle of the fight.

Bob Herring was first, within safe shooting distance
to save the dogs, and, waving his hand to those behind
him, he raised his rifle and sighted; but his favorite dog,
impatient for the report, anticipated it by jumping on
the bear, which, throwing up his head at the same instant, received the ball in his nose; at the crack of the
rifle—the well trained dogs, thinking less caution than
otherwise necessary, jumped pell-mell on the bear's
back, and the hardest fight ever witnessed in Summer
Retreat ensued; the hunter with Bob, placed his gun
almost against the bear's side, and the cap snapped—no

one else was near enough to fire without hitting the dogs.

"Give him the knife!" cried those at a distance.

Bob Herring's long blade was already flashing in his hand, but sticking a live bear is not child's play; he was standing undecided, when he saw the hind legs of Bose upwards; thrusting aside one or two of the dogs with his hand, he made a pass at the bear's throat, but the animal was so quick, that he struck the knife with his fore paw, and sent it whirling into the cane; another was instantly handed Bob, which he thrust at the bear, but the point was so blunt, that it would not penetrate the skin.

Foiled a third time, with a tremendous oath on himself, and the owner of a knife, "that wouldn't stick a cabbage," he threw it indignantly from him, and seizing, unceremoniously, a rifle, just then brought up by one of the party, heretofore in the rear; he, utterly regardless of his own legs, thrust it against the side of the bear with considerable force, and blowed him through; the bear struggled but for a moment, and fell dead.

"I saw snakes last night in my dreams," said Bob, handing back the rifle to its owner—"and I never had any good luck the next day, arter sich a sarcumstance— I call this hull hunt about as mean an affair as damp powder; that bar thar," pointing to the carcass, "that bar thar ought to have been killed afore he maimed a dog."

Then, speaking energetically, he said, " Boys, never fire at a bar's head, even if your iron is in his ear, its unsartain; look how I missed the brain, and only tore the smellers; with fewer dogs, and sich a shot, a fellow would be ripped open in a powder flash; and I say, cuss caps, and head shooting; they would have cost two lives to-day, but for them ar blessed dogs."

With such remarks Bob Herring beguiled away the time, while he, with others, skinned the bear. His huge carcass when dressed, though not over fat, looked like a huge young steer's. The dogs, as they recovered breath, partook of the refuse with a relish; the nearest possible route out of the Retreat was selected, and two horse loads took the meat into the open woods, where it was divided out in such a manner, that it could be taken home.

Bob Herring, while the dressing of the bear was going on, took the skin, and, on its inside surface, which glistened like satin, he carefully deposited the caul fat, and beside it the liver—the choice parts of the bear, according to the gourmand notions of the frontier, were in Bob's possession; and many years' experience had made him so expert in cooking it, that he was locally famed for this matter above all competitors.

It would be as impossible to give the recipe for this dish, so that it might be followed by the gastronomers of cities, as it would to have the articles composing it exposed for sale in the markets.

Bob Herring managed it as follows : he took a long wooden skewer, and having thrust its point through a small piece of the liver fat, he then followed it by a small piece of the liver, then the fat, then the liver, and so, on, until his most important material was consumed ; when this was done, he opened the " bear's handkerchief," or caul, and wrapped it round the whole, and thus roasted it before the fire. Like all the secrets in cookery, this dish depends, for its flavor and richness, upon giving exactly the proper quantities, as a superabundance of one, or the other, would completely spoil the dish.

"I was always unlucky, boys," said Bob—throwing the bear skin and its contents over his shoulders, " but I have had my fill often of caul fat and liver—many a man who thinks he's *lucky*, lives and dies as ignorant of its vartue, as a possum is of corn cake. If I ever look dead, boys, don't bury me until you see I don't open my eyes when the caul fat and liver is ready for eating ; if I don't move when you show me it, then I am a done goner, sure."

Night closed in before we reached our homes—the excitement of the morning wore upon our spirits and energy, but the evening's meal of caul fat and liver, and other " fixins," or Bob Herring's philosophical remarks,

restored me to perfect health, and I shall ever recollect
that supper, and its master of ceremonies, as harmo-
nious with, and as extraordinary as is, the " Summer
Retreat in Arkansas."

TOM OWEN.

TOM OWEN, THE BEE-HUNTER.

As a country becomes cleared up and settled, bee-hunters disappear, consequently they are seldom or never noticed beyond the immediate vicinity of their homes. Among this backwoods fraternity, have flourished men of genius, in their way, who have died unwept and unnoticed, while the heroes of the turf, and of the chase, have been lauded to the skies for every trivial superiority, they may have displayed in their respective pursuits.

To chronicle the exploits of sportsmen is commendable—the custom began as early as the days of the antediluvians, for we read, that "Nimrod was a mighty hunter before the Lord." Familiar, however, as Nimrod's name may be—or even Davy Crockett's—how unsatisfactory their records, when we reflect that TOM OWEN, the bee-hunter, is comparatively unknown?

Yes, the mighty Tom Owen has "hunted," from the

time that he could stand alone until the present time, and not a pen has inked paper to record his exploits. "Solitary and alone" has he traced his game through the mazy labyrinth of air; marked, I hunted;—I found; —I conquered;—upon the carcasses of his victims, and then marched homeward with his spoils: quietly and satisfiedly, sweetening his path through life; and, by its very obscurity, adding the principal element of the sublime.

It was on a beautiful southern October morning, at the hospitable mansion of a friend, where I was staying to drown dull care, that I first had the pleasure of seeing Tom Owen.

He was, on this occasion, straggling up the rising ground that led to the hospitable mansion of mine host, and the difference between him and ordinary men was visible at a glance; perhaps it showed itself as much in the perfect contempt of fashion that he displayed in the adornment of his outward man, as it did in the more elevated qualities of his mind, which were visible in his face. His head was adorned with an outlandish pattern of a hat—his nether limbs were encased by a pair of inexpressibles, beautifully fringed by the briar-bushes through which they were often drawn; coats and vests, he considered as superfluities; hanging upon his back were a couple of pails, and an axe in his right hand, formed the varieties that represented the corpus of Tom Owen.

As is usual with great men, he had his followers, who, with a courtier-like humility, depended upon the expression of his face for all their hopes of success.

The usual salutations of meeting were sufficient to draw me within the circle of his influence, and I at once became one of his most ready followers.

"See yonder!" said Tom, stretching his long arm into infinite space, "see yonder—there's a bee."

We all looked in the direction he pointed, but that was the extent of our observation.

"It was a fine bee," continued Tom, "black body, yellow legs, and went into that tree,"—pointing to a towering oak, blue in the distance. "In a clear day I can see a bee over a mile, easy!"

When did Coleridge "talk" like that? And yet Tom Owen uttered such a saying with perfect ease.

After a variety of meanderings through the thick woods, and clambering over fences, we came to our place of destination, as pointed out by Tom, who selected a mighty tree containing sweets, the possession of which the poets have likened to other sweets that leave a sting behind.

The felling of a mighty tree is a sight that calls up a variety of emotions; and Tom's game was lodged in one of the finest in the forest. But "the axe was laid at the root of the tree," which, in Tom's mind, was made expressly for bees to build their nests in, that he might cut them down, and obtain possession of their honeyed

3

treasure. The sharp axe, as it played in the hands of Tom, was replied to by a stout negro from the opposite side of the tree, and their united strokes fast gained upon the heart of their lordly victim.

There was little poetry in the thought, that long before this mighty empire of States was formed, Tom Owen's " bee-hive" had stretched its brawny arms to the winter's blast, and grown green in the summer's sun.

Yet such was the case, and how long I might have moralized I know not, had not the enraged buzzing about my ears satisfied me that the occupants of the tree were not going to give up their home and treasure, without showing considerable practical fight. No sooner had the little insects satisfied themselves that they were about to be invaded, than they began, one after another, to descend from their airy abode, and fiercely pitch into our faces; anon a small company, headed by an old veteran, would charge with its entire force upon all parts of our body at once.

It need not be said that the better part of valor was displayed by a precipitate retreat from such attacks.

In the midst of this warfare, the tree began to tremble with the fast-repeated strokes of the axe, and then might have been seen a "bee-line" of stingers precipitating themselves from above, on the unfortunate hunter beneath.

Now it was that Tom shone forth in his glory, for . his partisans—like many hangers-on about great men, began to desert him on the first symptoms of danger; and when the trouble thickened, they, one and all, took to their heels, and left only our hero and Sambo to fight the adversaries. Sambo, however, soon dropped his axe, and fell into all kinds of contortions; first he would seize the back of his neck with his hands, then his legs, and yell with pain. "Never holler till you get out of the woods," said the sublime Tom, consolingly; but writhe the negro did, until he broke, and left Tom "alone in his glory."

Cut,—thwack! sounded through the confused hum at the foot of the tree, marvellously reminding me of the interruptions that occasionally broke in upon the otherwise monotonous hours of my schoolboy days.

A sharp cracking finally told me the chopping was done, and, looking aloft, I saw the mighty tree balancing in the air. Slowly, and majestically, it bowed for the first time towards its mother earth,—gaining velocity as it descended, it shivered the trees that interrupted its downward course, and falling with thundering sound, splintered its mighty limbs, and buried them deeply in the ground.

The sun, for the first time in at least two centuries, broke uninterruptedly through the chasm made in the forest, and shone with splendor upon the magnificent Tom, standing a conqueror among his spoils.

As might be expected, the bees were very much astonished and confused, and by their united voices proclaimed death, had it been in their power, to all their foes, not, of course, excepting Tom Owen himself. But the wary hunter was up to the tricks of his trade, and, like a politician, he knew how easily an enraged mob could be quelled with smoke; and smoke he tried, until his enemies were completely destroyed.

We, Tom's hangers-on, now approached his treasure. It was a rich one, and, as he observed, "contained a rich chance of plunder." Nine feet, by measurement, of the hollow of the tree was full, and this afforded many pails of pure honey.

Tom was liberal, and supplied us all with more than we wanted, and "toted," by the assistance of Sambo, his share to his own home, soon to be devoured, and soon to be replaced by the destruction of another tree, and another nation of bees.

Thus Tom exhibited within himself an unconquerable genius which would have immortalized him, had he directed it in following the sports of Long Island or New Market.

We have seen the great men of the southern turf glorying around the victories of their favorite sport,— we have heard the great western hunters detail the soul-stirring adventures of a bear-hunt—we have listened, with almost suffocating interest, to the tale of a Nantucket seaman, while he portrayed the death of a mighty whale—and we have also seen Tom Owen triumphantly engaged in a bee-hunt—we beheld and wondered at the sports of the turf—the field—and the sea—because the objects acted on by man were terrible, indeed, when their instincts were aroused.

But, in the bee-hunt of Tom Owen, and its consummation,—the grandeur *visible* was imparted by the mighty mind of Tom Owen himself.

ARROW-FISHING.

In treating of the most beautiful and novel sport of arrow-fishing, its incidents are so interwoven with ten thousand accessories, that we scarce know how to separate our web, without either breaking it, or destroying a world of interest hidden among the wilds of the American forest.

The lakes over which the arrow-fisher twangs his bow, in the pleasant spring-time; have disappeared long before the sere and yellow leaf of autumn appears, and the huntsman's horn, and the loud-mouthed pack, clamor melodiously after the scared deer upon their bottoms.

To explain this phenomenon, the lover of nature must follow us until we exhibit some of the vagaries of the great Mississippi, and, having fairly got our "flood and field" before us, we will engage heartily in the sport.

If you will descend with me from slightly broken ground through which we have been riding, covered with forest trees singularly choked up with undergrowth, to an expanse of country beautifully open between the trees, the limbs of which start out from the trunk some thirty feet above the ground, you will find at your feet an herbage that is luxuriant, but scanty; high over your head, upon the trees, you will perceive *a line*, marking what has evidently been an overflow of water; you can trace the beautiful level upon the trunks of the trees, as far as the eye can reach.

It is in the fall of the year, and a squirrel drops an acorn upon your shoulder, and about your feet are the sharp-cut tracks of the nimble deer. You are standing in the centre of what is called, by hunters, a " dry lake."

As the warm air of April favors the opening flowers of spring, the waters of the Mississippi, increased by the melting snows of the North, swell within its low banks, and rush in a thousand streams back into the swamps and lowlands that lie upon its borders; the torrent sweeps along into the very reservoir in which we stand, and the waters swell upwards until they find a level with the fountain itself. Thus is formed the ar- row-fisher's lake.

The brawny oak, the graceful pecan, the tall poplar, and delicate beech spring from its surface in a thousand tangled limbs, looking more beautiful, yet most unnat-

ural, as the water reflects them downwards, hiding completely away their submerged trunks.   The arrow-fisher
now peeps in the nest of the wild bird from his little
boat, and runs its prow plump into the hollow, that
marks the doorway of some cunning squirrel.

In fact, he navigates for awhile his bark where, in
the fall of the year, the gay-plumed songster and the
hungry hawk plunge mid-air, and float not more swiftly
nor gayly, on light pinioned wings, than he in his swift
canoe.

A chapter from nature : and who unfolds the great
book so understandingly, and learns so truly from its
wisdom, as the piscator ?

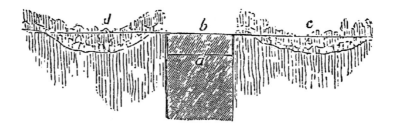

a, The level of the Mississippi, at its ordinary stage of water.
b, The height of the spring rise.   *c, d*, The "dry lakes."   By examination of the above drawing, an idea may be formed of the
manner of the rises of the Mississippi.   The observer will notice
that when the water is at *a*, the lakes *c* and *d* will be *dry*, affording a fine hunting-ground for deer, &c.   When the water is at
b, the lakes are formed, and arrow-fishing is pursued.   (See description.)   A correct idea may also be formed by what is meant
by a *water-line* on the trees, indicating the last rise ; the water-
line will be formed of the sediment settling on the trees at the
line *b*, marked above.

The rippling brook, as it dances along in the sunshine, bears with it the knowledge, there is truthfulness in water, though it be not in a well. We can find something, if we will, to love and admire under every wave; and the noises of every tiny brook are tongues that speak eloquently to nature's true priests.

We have marked, that with the rise of the waters, the fish grow gregarious, and that they rush along in schools *with the waters that flow inland* from the river, —they thus choose these temporary sylvan lakes as depositories of their spawn; thus wittingly providing against that destruction that would await their young, in the highways of their journeyings.

It is a sight to wonder at, in the wilds of the primitive forest, to see the fish rushing along the narrow inlets, with the current, in numbers incredible to the imagination, leaping over the fallen tree that is only half buried in the surface of the stream, or stayed a moment in their course by the meshes of the strong net, either bursting it by force of numbers, or granting its wasteful demands by thousands, without seemingly to diminish the multitude, more than a single leaf taken from the forest would perceptibly alter the vegetation.

We have marked, too, that these fish would besport themselves in their new homes, secluding themselves in the shadows of the trees and banks; and, as the summer heats come on, they would grow unquiet; the outlets leading to the great river they had left would be

3*

thronged by what seemed to be busy couriers; and when the news finally spread of *falling water*, one night would suffice to make the lake, before so thronged with finny life, deserted; and a few nights only, perhaps, would pass, when the narrow bar would intrude itself between the inland lake and the river, that supplied it with water.

Such was the fish's wisdom, seen and felt, where man, with his learning and his nicely-wrought mechanisms, would watch in vain the air, the clouds, and see "no signs" of falling water.*

Among arrow-fishermen there are technicalities, an understanding of which will give a more ready idea of the sport. The surfaces of these inland lakes are un-ruffled by the winds or storms; the heats of the sun seem to rest upon them; they are constantly sending into the upper regions, warm mists. Their surfaces,

---

* It may not be uninteresting to naturalists to be informed, that these fish run into the inland lakes to spawn, and they do it of course with the rise of the water. These overflows are annual. A few years since the season was very singular, and there were *three* distinct rises and falls of water, and at each rise the fish followed the water inland, and spawned: a remarkable example where the usual order of nature was reversed in one instance, and yet continuing blindly consistent in another. It is also very remarkable that the young fish, native of the lakes, are as interested to mark the indications of falling water as those that come into them; and in a long series of years of observation, but one fall was ever known before the fish had left the lakes.

however, are covered with innumerable bubbles, either floating about, or breaking into little circling ripples.

To the superficial observer, these air-bubbles mean little or nothing; to the arrow-fisherman they are the very *language of his art;* visible writing upon the unstable water, unfolding the secrets of the depths below, and guiding him, with unerring certainty, in his pursuits.

Seat yourself quietly in this little skiff, and while I paddle quietly out into the lake, I will translate to you these apparent wonders, and give you a lesson in the simple language of nature.

" An air-bubble is an air-bubble," you say, and " your fine distinctions must be in the imagination."

Well! then mark how stately ascends that large globule of air; if you will time each succeeding one by your watch, you will find that while they appear, it is at regular intervals, and when they burst upon the surface of the water, there is the least spray in the world sparkling for an instant in the sun. Now, yonder, if you will observe, are very minute bubbles that seem to *simmer* towards the surface. Could you catch the air of the first bubble we noticed, and give it to an ingenious chemist, he would tell you that it was a light gas, that exhaled from decaying vegetable matter.

The arrow-fisherman will tell you that it comes from an old stump, and is denominated a *dead bubble.* That " simmering " was made by some comfortable turtle, as he opened his mouth and gave his breath to the surrounding element.

Look ahead of you: when did you ever see an Archimedean screw more beautifully marked out than by that group of bubbles? They are very light, indeed, and seem thus gracefully to struggle into the upper world; they denote the eager workings of some terrapin in the soft mud at the bottom of the lake. In the shade of yonder lusty oak, you will perceive what arrow-fishermen call a "feed;" you see that the bubbles are entirely unlike any we have noticed; they come rushing upwards swiftly, like handfuls of silver shot. They are lively and animated to look at, and are caused by the fish below, as they, around the root of that very oak, search for insects for food. To those bubbles the arrow-fisherman hastens for game; they are made by the fish that he calls legitimate for his sport.

In early spring the fish are discovered, not only by the bubbles they make, but by various sounds, uttered while searching for food. These sounds are familiarized, and betray the kind of fish that make them. In late spring, from the middle of May to June, the fish come near the surface of the water, and expose their mouths to the air, keeping up, at the same time, a constant motion with it, called " piping."

Fish thus exposed are in groups, and are called a "float." The cause of this phenomenon is hard to explain, all reasons given being unsatisfactory. As it is only exhibited in the hottest of weather, it may be best accounted for in the old verse :

> " The sun, from its perpendicular height,
>   Illumined the depths of the sea;
> The fishes, beginning to sweat,
>   Cry, 'Dang it, how hot we shall be!'"

There are several kinds of fish that attract the attention of the arrow-fishermen. Two kinds only are professedly pursued, the "carp" and the "buffalo." Several others, however, are attacked for the mere purpose of amusement, among which we may mention a species of perch, and the most extraordinary of all fish, the " gar."

The carp is a fish known to all anglers. Its habits must strike every one familiar with them, as being eminently in harmony with the retreats we have described. In these lakes they vary in weight from five to thirty pounds, and are preferred by arrow-fishermen to all other fish.

The " buffalo," a sort of fresh-water sheep's-head, is held next in estimation. A species of perch is also taken, that vary from three to ten pounds, in weight; but as they are full of bones and coarse in flesh, they are killed simply to test the skill of the arrow-fisherman.*

* The carp, to which we allude, is so accurately described in its habits in "Blane's Encyclopedia of Rural Sports," when

The incredible increase of fishes has been a matter of immemorial observation. In the retired lakes and streams we speak of, but for a wise arrangement of Providence, it seems not improbable that they would outgrow the very space occupied by the element in which they exist. To prevent this consummation, there are fresh water fiends, more terrible than the wolves and tigers of the land, that prowl on the finny tribe, with an appetite commensurate with their plentifulness, destroying millions in a day, yet leaving, from their abundance, untold numbers to follow their habits and the cycle of their existence undisturbed. These terrible destroyers have no true representatives in the sea; they seem to be peculiar to waters tributary to the Mississippi.

speaking of the European carp, that we are tempted to make one or two extracts that are remarkable for their truthfulness as applied to the section of the United States where arrow-fishing is a sport. In the work we allude to, we have the following:

"The usual length of the carp in our own country (England) is from about twelve to fifteen or sixteen inches; but *in warm climates*, it often arrives at the length of two, three, or four feet, and to the weight of twenty, thirty, or even forty pounds." Par. 3448. Again, "The haunts of the carp of stagnant water are, during the spring and autumn months, in the deepest parts, particularly near the flood-gates by which water *is received and let off*. In the summer months they frequent the weed beds, and *come near to the surface*, and particularly are fond of aquatic plants, which spring from the bottom and rise to the top." Par. 3453. We find that the fish retains the same distinctive habits in both hemispheres, altering only from the peculiarities of the

There are two kinds of them, alike in office, but distinct in species; they are known by those who fish in the streams which they inhabit as the "gar." They are, when grown to their full size, twelve or fifteen feet in length, voracious monsters to look at, so well made for strength, so perfectly protected from assault, so capable of inflicting injury. The smaller kind, growing not larger than six feet, have a body that somewhat resembles in form the pike, covered by what looks more like large, flat heads of wrought iron, than scales, which it is impossible to remove without cutting them out—they are so deeply imbedded in the flesh. The jaws of this monster, form about one fourth of its whole length; they are shaped like the bill of a goose, armed in the interior with triple rows of teeth, as sharp, and well set, as those of a saw.

But *the terror*, is the "alligator gar," a monster that seems to combine all the most destructive powers of the shark and the reptile. The alligator gar grows to the enormous length of fifteen feet; its head resembles the alligator's; within its wide-extended jaws glisten innumerable rows of teeth, running, in solid columns, down into its very throat. Blind in its instinct to destroy, and singularly tenacious of life, it seems to prey with untiring energy, and with an appetite that is increased by gratification.

Such are the fish, that are made victims of the mere sport of the arrow-fisherman.

The implements of the arrow-fisherman are a strong bow, five or six feet long, made of black locust or of cedar (the latter being preferred), and an arrow of ash, three feet long, pointed with an iron spear of peculiar construction. The spear is eight inches long, one end has a socket, in which is fitted *loosely* the wooden shaft; the other end is a flattened point; back of this point there is inserted the barb, which shuts into the iron as it enters an object, but will open if attempted to be drawn out. The whole of this iron-work weighs three ounces. A cord, about the size of a crow-quill, fifteen or twenty feet long, is attached to the spear, by which is held the fish when struck.

Of the water-craft used in arrow-fishing, much might be said, as it introduces the common Indian canoe, or as it is familiarly termed, the "dug out," which is nothing more than a trunk of a tree, shaped according to the humor or taste of its artificer, and hollowed out.

We have seen some of these rude barks that claimed but one degree of beauty or utility beyond the common log, and we have seen others as gracefully turned as was ever the bosom of the loving swan, and that would, as gracefully as Leda's bird, spring through the rippling waves.

The arrow-fisher prefers a canoe with very little rake, quite flat on the bottom, and not more than fifteen feet long, so as to be quickly turned. Place in this simple craft the simpler paddle, lay beside it the arrow, the bow, the cord, and you have the whole outfit of the ar-row-fisherman.

To the uninitiated, the guidance of a canoe is a mystery. The grown-up man, who first attempts to move on skates over the glassy ice, has a command of his limbs, and a power of locomotion, that the novice in canoe navigation has not. Never at rest, it seems to rush from under his feet; overbalanced by an overdrawn breath, it precipitates its victim into the water. Every effort renders it more and more unmanageable, until it is condemned as worthless.

But, let a person accustomed to its movements take it in charge, and it gayly launches into the stream; whether standing or sitting, the master has it entirely under his control, moving any way with a quickness, a pliability, quite wonderful, forward, sideways, backwards; starting off in an instant, or while at the greatest speed, instantly stopping still, and doing all this more perfectly, than with any other water-craft of the world.

In arrow-fishing, two persons are only employed; each one has his work designated—"the paddler" and "bowman."

Before the start is made, a perfect understanding is

had, so that their movements are governed by signs.
The delicate canoe is pushed into the lake, its occupants
scarcely breathe to get it balanced, the paddler is seated
in its bottom, near its centre, where he remains, governing the canoe in all its motions, without *ever taking the
paddle from the water.*

The fisherman stands at the bow; around the wrist
of his left hand is fastened, by a loose loop, the cord attached to the arrow, which cord is wound around the
forefinger of the same hand, so that when paying off, it
will do so easily. In the same hand is, of course, held
the bow. In the right is carried the arrow, and, by its
significant pointing, the paddler gives directions for the
movements of the canoe.

The craft glides along, scarcely making a ripple; a
" feed " is discovered, over which the canoe stops; the
bowman draws his arrow to the head; the game, disturbed, is seen in the clear water rising slowly and perpendicularly, but otherwise perfectly motionless; the
arrow speeds its way; in an instant the shaft shoots
into the air, and floats quietly away, while the wounded
fish, carrying the spear in its body, endeavours to
escape.

The " pull " is managed so as to come directly from
the bow of the canoe; it lasts but for a moment before
the transfixed fish is seen, fins playing, and full of ago-
nizing life, dancing on the top of the water, and in another instant more lies dead at the bottom of the canoe.

" The bowman draws his arrow to the head."—*page* 66.

The shaft is then gone after, picked up, and thrust into the spear; the cord is again adjusted, and the canoe moves towards the merry makers of those swift ascending bubbles, so brightly displaying themselves on the edge of that deep shade, cast by yonder evergreen oak.

There is much in the associations of arrow-fishing that gratifies taste, and makes it partake of a refined and intellectual character. Beside the knowledge it gives of the character of fishes, it practises one in the curious refractions of water. Thus will the arrow-fisherman, from long experience, drive his pointed shaft a fathom deep for game, when it would seem, to the novice, that a few inches would be more than sufficient.

Again, the waters that supply the arrow-fisherman with game, afford subsistence to innumerable birds, and he has exhibited before him, the most beautiful displays of their devices to catch the finny tribe.

The kingfisher may be seen the livelong day, acting a prominent part, bolstering up its fantastic topknot, as if to apologize for a manifest want of neck; you can hear him always scolding and clamorous among the low brush, and overhanging limits of trees, eyeing the minnows as they glance along the shore, and making vain essays to fasten them in his bill.

The hawk, too, often swoops down from the clouds, swift as the bolt of Jove; the cleft air whistles in the flight; the sportive fish, playing in the sunlight, is snatched up in the rude talons, and borne aloft, the reeking water from its scaly sides falling in soft spray upon the upturned eye that traces its daring course. But we treat of fish, and not of birds.

Yonder is our canoe; the paddle has stopped it short, just where you see those faint bubbles; the water is very deep beneath them, and reflects the frail bark and its occupants, as clearly as if they were floating in mid air. The bowman looks into the water—the fish are out of sight, and not disturbed by the intrusion above them. They are eating busily, judging from the ascending bubbles.

The bowman lets fall the "heel" of his arrow on the bottom of the canoe, and the bubbles instantly cease. The slight tap has made a great deal of noise in the water, though scarcely heard out of it. There can be seen rising to the surface a tremendous carp. How quietly it comes upwards, its pectoral fins playing like the wings of the sportive butterfly. Another moment, and the cold iron is in its body.

Paralyzed for an instant, the fish rises to the surface as if dead, then, recovering itself, it rushes downwards, until the cord that holds it prisoner tightens, and makes the canoe tremble; the effort has destroyed it, and without another struggle it is secured.

When the fish first come into the lakes, they move in pairs on the surface of the water, and while so doing they are shot, as it is called, "flying."

In early spring fifteen or twenty fish are secured in

an hour. As the season advances, three or four taken in the same length of time, is considered quite good success.

To stand upon the shore, and see the arrow-fisherman busily employed, is a very interesting exhibition of skill, and of the picturesque. The little "dug out" seems animate with intelligence; the bowman draws his long shaft, you see it enter the water, and then follows the glowing sight of the fine fish sparkling in the sun, as if sprinkled with diamonds.

At times, too, when legitimate sport tires, some ravenous gar that heaves in sight, is made a victim; aim is taken just ahead of his dorsal fin; secured, he flounders a while, and then drags off the canoe as if in harness, skimming it almost out of the water with his speed. Fatigued, finally, with his useless endeavours to escape, he will rise to the surface, open his huge mouth, and gasp for air. The water that streams from his jaws will be colored with blood from the impaled fish that still struggle in the terrors of his barbed teeth. Rushing ahead again, he will, by eccentric movements, try the best skill of the paddler to keep his canoe from overturning into the lake, a consummation not always unattained. The gar finally dies, and is dragged ashore; this buzzard revels on his carcass, and every piscator contemplates, with disgust, the great enemy to his game, this terrible monarch of the fresh-water seas.

The crumbling character of the alluvial banks that

line our southern streams, the quantity of fallen timber, the amount of " snags" and " sawyers," and the great plentifulness of game, make the beautiful art of angling, as pursued in our Northern States, impossible.

The veriest tyro, who finds a delicate reed in every nook that casts a shadow in the water, with his rough line, and coarser hook, *can catch fish.* The greedy perch, in all its beautiful varieties, swim eagerly and swiftly around the snare, and swallow it, without suspicion that a worm is not a worm, or that appearances are ever deceitful. The jointed rod, the scientific reel, cannot be used; the thick hanging bough, the rank grass, the sunken log, the far reaching *melumbium,* the ever still water, make these delicate appliances useless.

Arrow-fishing only, of all the angling in the interior streams of the southwest, comparatively speaking, claims the title of *an art,* as it is pursued with a skill and a thorough knowledge that tell only with the experienced, and to the novice, is an impossibility.

The originators of arrow-fishing deserve the credit of striking out a rare and beautiful amusement, when the difficulties of securing their game did not require it, showing that it resulted in the spirit of true sport alone.

The origin of arrow-fishing we know not; the country where it is pursued is comparatively of recent settlement; scarce three generations have passed away within its boundaries.

We asked the oldest piscator that lived in the vicinity of these " dry lakes," for information regarding the early history of arrow-fishing, and he told us, that it was " invented by old Uncle Zac," and gave us his history in a brief and pathetic manner, concluding his reminiscences of the great departed, as follows :

" Uncle Zac never know'd nothing 'bout flies, or tickling trout, but it took *him* to tell the difference 'twixt a yarth worm, a grub, or the young of a wasp's nest ; in fact, he know'd fishes amazin', and bein' natur-ally a hunter, he went to shooten 'em with a bow and arrer, to keep up yerly times in his history, when he tuck Inguns and other varmints, in the same way."

THE BIG BEAR OF ARKANSAS.

A STEAMBOAT on the Mississippi, frequently, in making her regular trips, carries between places varying from one to two thousand miles apart; and, as these boats advertise to land passengers and freight at "all intermediate landings," the heterogeneous character of the passengers of one of these up-country boats can scarcely be imagined by one who has never seen it with his own eyes.

Starting from New Orleans in one of these boats, you will find yourself associated with men from every State in the Union, and from every portion of the globe; and a man of observation need not lack for amusement or instruction in such a crowd, if he will take the trouble to read the great book of character so favorably opened before him.

Here may be seen, jostling together, the wealthy

The Big Bear of Arkansas.

Southern planter and the pedler of tin-ware from New England—the Northern merchant and the Southern jockey—a venerable bishop, and a desperate gambler— the land speculator, and the honest farmer—professional men of all creeds and characters—Wolvereens, Suckers, Hoosiers, Buckeyes, and Corncrackers, beside a "plentiful sprinkling" of the half-horse and half-alligator species of men, who are peculiar to "old Mississippi," and who appear to gain a livelihood by simply going up and down the river. In the pursuit of pleasure or business, I have frequently found myself in such a crowd.

On one occasion, when in New Orleans, I had occasion to take a trip of a few miles up the Mississippi, and I hurried on board the well-known "high-pressure-and-beat-every-thing" steamboat "Invincible," just as the last note of the last bell was sounding; and when the confusion and bustle that is natural to a boat's getting under way had subsided, I discovered that I was associated in as heterogeneous a crowd as was ever got together. As my trip was to be of a few hours' duration only, I made no endeavors to become acquainted with my fellow-passengers, most of whom would be together many days. Instead of this, I took out of my pocket the "latest paper," and more critically than usual examined its contents; my fellow-passengers, at the same time, disposed of themselves in little groups.

While I was thus busily employed in reading, and my companions were more busily still employed, in

4

discussing such subjects as suited their humors best, we were most unexpectedly startled by a loud Indian whoop, uttered in the "social hall," that part of the cabin fitted off for a bar; then was to be heard a loud crowing, which would not have continued to interest us —such sounds being quite common in that *place of spirits*—had not the hero of these windy accomplishments stuck his head into the cabin, and hallooed out, "Hurra for the Big Bear of Arkansaw!"

Then might be heard a confused hum of voices, unintelligible, save in such broken sentences as "horse," "screamer," "lightning is slow," &c.

As might have been expected, this continued interruption, attracted the attention of every one in the cabin; all conversation ceased, and in the midst of this surprise, the "Big Bear" walked into the cabin, took a chair, put his feet on the stove, and looking back over his shoulder, passed the general and familiar salute—"Strangers, how are you?"

He then expressed himself as much at home as if he had been at "the Forks of Cypress," and "prehaps a little more so."

Some of the company at this familiarity looked a little angry, and some astonished; but in a moment every face was wreathed in a smile. There was something about the intruder that won the heart on sight. He appeared to be a man enjoying perfect health and contentment; his eyes were as sparkling as diamonds,

and good-natured to simplicity. Then his perfect confidence in himself was irresistibly droll.

"Prehaps," said he, "gentlemen," running on without
a person interrupting, "prehaps you have been to New
Orleans often ; I never made *the first visit before*, and
I don't intend to make another in a crow's life. I am
thrown away in that ar place, and useless, that ar a fact.
Some of the gentlemen thar called me *green*—well, prehaps I am, said I, *but I arn't so at home ;* and if I aint
off my trail much, the heads of them perlite chaps themselves wern't much the hardest; for according to my
notion, they were *real know-nothings*, green as a pump-
kin-vine—couldn't, in farming, I'll bet, raise a crop of
turnips; and as for shooting, they'd miss a barn if the
door was swinging, and that, too, with the best rifle in
the country. And then they talked to me 'bout hunting, and laughed at my calling the principal game in
Arkansaw poker, and high-low-jack.

"'Prehaps,' said I, 'you prefer checkers and roulette;'
at this they laughed harder than ever, and asked me if
I lived in the woods, and didn't know what *game* was?

"At this, I rather think *I* laughed.

"'Yes,' I roared, and says, I, 'Strangers, if you'd
asked me *how we got our meat* in Arkansaw, I'd a told
you at once, and given you a list of varmints that would
make a caravan, beginning with the bar, and ending off
with the cat; that's *meat* though, not game.

"Game, indeed,—that's what city folks call it; and

with them it means chippen-birds and shite-pokes ; may be such trash live in my diggins, but I arn't noticed them yet : a bird anyway is too trifling. I never did shoot at but one, and I'd never forgiven myself for that, had it weighed less than forty pounds. I wouldn't draw a rifle on any thing less heavy than that; and when I meet with another wild turkey of the same size, I will drap him."

" A wild turkey weighing forty pounds !" exclaimed twenty voices in the cabin at once.

" Yes, strangers, and wasn't it a whopper ? You see, the thing was so fat that it couldn't fly far ; and when he fell out of the tree, after I shot him, on striking the ground he bust open behind, and the way the pound gobs of tallow rolled out of the opening was perfectly beautiful."

" Where did all that happen ? " asked a cynical-looking Hoosier.

" Happen ! happened in Arkansaw : where else could it have happened, but in the creation State, the finishing-up country—a State where the *sile* runs down to the centre of the 'arth, and government gives you a title to every inch of it ? Then its airs—just breathe them, and they will make you snort like a horse. It's a State without a fault, it is."

" Excepting mosquitoes," cried the Hoosier.

" Well, stranger, except them; for it ar a fact that they are rather *enormous*, and do push themselves in somewhat troublesome. But, stranger, they never stick twice in the same place; and give them a fair chance for a few months, and you will get as much above no-ticing them as an alligator. They can't hurt my feel-ings, for they lay under the skin; and I never knew but one case of injury resulting from them, and that was to a Yankee: and they take worse to foreigners, any how, than they do to natives. But the way they used that fellow up! first they punched him until he swelled up and busted; then he sup-per-a-ted, as the doctor called it, until he was as raw as beef; then, owing to the warm weather, he tuck the ager, and finally he tuck a steamboat and left the country. He was the only man that ever tuck mosquitoes at heart that I knowd of.

"But mosquitoes is natur, and I never find fault with her. If they ar large, Arkansaw is large, her var-mints ar large, her trees ar large, her rivers ar large, and a small mosquito would be of no more use in Ar-kansaw than preaching in a cane-brake."

This knock-down argument in favor of big mos-quitoes used the Hoosier up, and the logician started on a new track, to explain how numerous bear were in his "diggins," where he represented them to be "about as plenty as blackberries, and a little plentifuller."

Upon the utterance of this assertion, a timid little man near me inquired, if the bear in Arkansaw ever attacked the settlers in numbers?

"No," said our hero, warming with the subject, "no,

stranger, for you see it ain't the natur of bear to go in droves; but the way they squander about in pairs and single ones is edifying.

"And then the way I hunt them—the old black ras- cals know the crack of my gun as well as they know a pig's squealing. They grow thin in our parts, it fright- ens them so, and they do take the noise dreadfully, poor things. That gun of mine is a perfect *epidemic among bear:* if not watched closely, it will go off as quick on a warm scent as my dog Bowieknife will: and then that dog—whew! why the fellow thinks that the world is full of bear, he finds them so easy. It's lucky he don't talk as well as think; for with his natural modesty, if he should suddenly learn how much he is acknowledged to be ahead of all other dogs in the universe, he would be astonished to death in two minutes.

"Strangers, that dog knows a bear's way as well as a horse-jockey knows a woman's: he always barks at the right time, bites at the exact place, and whips without getting a scratch.

"I never could tell whether he was made expressly to hunt bear, or whether bear was made expressly for him to hunt; any way, I believe they were ordained to go together as naturally as Squire Jones says a man and woman is, when he moralizes in marrying a couple. In fact, Jones once said, said he, 'Marriage according to law is a civil contract of divine origin; it's common to all countries as well as Arkansaw, and people take to it as naturally as Jim Doggett's Bowieknife takes to bear.' "

"What season of the year do your hunts take place?" inquired a gentlemanly foreigner, who, from some peculiarities of his baggage, I suspected to be an Englishman, on some hunting expedition, probably at the foot of the Rocky Mountains.

"The season for bear hunting, stranger," said the man of Arkansaw, "is generally all the year round, and the hunts take place about as regular. I read in history that varmints have their fat season, and their lean season. That is not the case in Arkansaw, feeding as they do upon the *spontenacious* productions of the sile, they have one continued fat season the year round; though in winter things in this way is rather more greasy than in summer, I must admit. For that reason bear with us run in warm weather, but in winter they only waddle.

"Fat, fat! its an enemy to speed; it tames every thing that has plenty of it. I have seen wild turkeys, from its influence, as gentle as chickens. Run a bear in this fat condition, and the way it improves the critter for eating is amazing; it sort of mixes the ile up with the meat, until you can't tell t'other from which. I've done this often.

"I recollect one perty morning in particular, of putting an old he fellow on the stretch, and considering the weight he carried, he run well. But the dogs soon

tired him down, and when I came up with him wasn't
he in a beautiful sweat—I might say fever; and then to
see his tongue sticking out of his mouth a feet, and his
sides sinking and opening like a bellows, and his cheeks
so fat that he couldn't look cross. In this fix I blazed
at him, and pitch me naked into a briar patch, if the
steam didn't come out of the bullet-hole ten foot in a
straight line. The fellow, I reckon, was made on the
high-pressure system, and the lead sort of bust his
biler."

"That column of steam was rather curious, or else
the bear must have been very *warm*," observed the foreigner, with a laugh.

"Stranger, as you observe, that bear was WARM, and
the blowing off of the steam show'd it, and also how hard
the varmint had been run. I have no doubt if he had
kept on two miles farther his insides would have been
stewed; and I expect to meet with a varmint yet of extra bottom, that will run himself into a skinfull of bear's
grease: it is possible; much onlikelier things have
happened."

"Whereabouts are these bears so abundant?" inquired the foreigner, with increasing interest.

"Why, stranger, they inhabit the neighborhood of
my settlement, one of the prettiest places on old Mississipp—a perfect location, and no mistake; a place
that had some defects until the river made the ' cut-off '
at ' Shirt-tail bend,' and that remedied the evil, as it

brought my cabin on the edge of the river—a great advantage in wet weather, I assure you, as you can now roll a barrel of whiskey into my yard in high water from a boat, as easy as falling off a log. It's a great improvement, as toting it by land in a jug, as I used to do, *evaporated* it too fast, and it became expensive.

" Just stop with me, stranger, a month or two, or a year, if you like, and you will appreciate my place. I can give you plenty to eat; for beside hog and hominy, you can have bear-ham, and bear-sausages, and a mattrass of bear-skins to sleep on, and a wildcat-skin, pulled off hull, stuffed with corn-shucks, for a pillow. That bed would put you to sleep if you had the rheumatics in every joint in your body. I call that ar bed, a *quietus*.

"Then look at my ' pre-emption '—the government aint got another like it to dispose of. Such timber, and such bottom land,—why you can't preserve any thing natural you plant in it unless you pick it young, things thar will grow out of shape so quick.

I once planted in those diggins a few potatoes and beets; they took a fine start, and after that, an ox team couldn't have kept them from growing. About that time I went off to old Kaintuck on business, and did not hear from them things in three months, when I accidentally stumbled on a fellow who had drapped in at my place, with an idea of buying me out.

" ' How did you like things ? ' said I.

" ' Pretty well,' said he; ' the cabin is convenient,

and the timber land is good ; but that bottom land aint worth the first red cent.' "

" ' Why ? ' said I.

" ' 'Cause,' said he.

" ' 'Cause what ? ' said I.

" ' 'Cause it's full of cedar stumps and Indian mounds, and *can't be cleared.*'

" ' Lord,' said I, ' them ar " cedar stumps " is beets, and them ar " Indian mounds " tater hills.'

" As I had expected, the crop was overgrown and use-less : the sile is too rich, *and planting in Arkansaw is dangerous.*

" I had a good-sized sow killed in that same bottom-land. The old thief stole an ear of corn, and took it down to eat where she slept at night. Well, she left a grain or two on the ground, and lay down on them : before morning the corn shot up, and the percussion killed her dead. I don't plant any more : natur intended Arkansaw for a hunting ground, and I go according to natur."

The questioner, who had thus elicited the description of our hero's settlement, seemed to be perfectly satis-fied, and said no more ; but the " Big Bear of Arkansaw " rambled on from one thing to another with a volubility perfectly astonishing, occasionally disputing with those around him, particularly with a " live Sucker " from Illinois, who had the daring to say that our Arkansaw friend's stories " smelt rather tall."

The evening was nearly spent by the incidents we have detailed; and conscious that my own association with so singular a personage would probably end before morning, I asked him if he would not give me a description of some particular bear hunt; adding, that I took great interest in such things, though I was no sportsman. The desire seemed to please him, and he squared himself round towards me, saying, that he could give me an idea of a bear hunt that was never beat in this world, or in any other. His manner was so singular, that half of his story consisted in his excellent way of telling it, the great peculiarity of which was, the happy manner he had of emphasizing the prominent parts of his conversation. As near as I can recollect, I have italicized the words, and given the story in his own way.

"Stranger," said he, "in bear hunts *I am numerous*, and which particular one, as you say, I shall tell, puzzles me.

"There was the old she devil I shot at the Hurricane last fall—then there was the old hog thief I popped over at the Bloody Crossing, and then—Yes, I have it! I will give you an idea of a hunt, in which the greatest bear was killed that ever lived, *none excepted ;* about an old fellow that I hunted, more or less, for two or three years; and if that aint a *particular bear hunt,* I ain't got one to tell.

"But in the first place, stranger, let me say, I am pleased with you, because you aint ashamed to gain in-

formation by asking and listening; and that's what I
say to Countess's pups every day when I'm home; and
I have got great hopes of them ar pups, because they are
continually *nosing* about ; and though they stick it
sometimes in the wrong place, they gain experience any
how, and may learn something useful to boot.

"Well, as I was saying about this big bear, you see
when I and some more first settled in our region, we
were drivin to hunting naturally ; we soon liked it, and
after that we found it an easy matter to make the thing
our business.   One old chap who had pioneered 'afore
us, gave us to understand that we had settled in the
right place.   He dwelt upon its merits until it was affecting, and showed us, to prove his assertions, more
scratches on the bark of the sassafras trees, than I ever
saw chalk marks on a tavern door 'lection time.

" ' Who keeps that ar reckoning ? ' said I.

" ' The bear,' said he.

" ' What for ? ' said I.

" ' Can't tell,' said he; 'but so it is : the bear bite
the bark and wood too, at the highest point from the
ground they can reach, and you can tell, by the marks,'
said he, ' the length of the bear to an inch.'

" ' Enough,' said I ; ' I've learned something here
a'ready, and I'll put it in practice.'

" Well, stranger, just one month from that time I
killed a bar, and told its exact length before I measured

it, by those very marks; and when I did that, I swelled up considerably—I've been a prouder man ever since.

"So I went on, larning something every day, until I was reckoned a buster, and allowed to be decidedly the best bear hunter in my district; and that is a reputation as much harder to earn than to be reckoned first man in Congress, as an iron ramrod is harder than a toadstool.

"Do the varmints grow over-cunning by being fooled with by greenhorn hunters, and by this means get troublesome, they send for me, as a matter of course; and thus I do my own hunting, and most of my neighbors'. I walk into the varmints though, and it has become about as much the same to me as drinking. It is told in two sentences—

"A bear is started, and he is killed.

"The thing is somewhat monotonous now—I know just how much they will run, where they will tire, how much they will growl, and what a thundering time I will have in getting their meat home. I could give you the history of the chase with all the particulars at the commencement, I know the signs so well—*Stranger, I'm certain.* Once I met with a match, though, and I will tell you about it; for a common hunt would not be worth relating.

"On a fine fall day, long time ago, I was trailing about for bear, and what should I see but fresh marks on the sassafras trees, about eight inches above any in the forests that I knew of. Says I, 'Them marks is a hoax, or it indicates the d——t bear that was ever grown.' In fact, stranger, I couldn't believe it was real, and I went on. Again I saw the same marks, at the same height, and *I knew the thing lived.* That conviction came home to my soul like an earthquake.

"Says I, 'Here is something a-purpose for me : that bear is mine, or I give up the hunting business.' The very next morning, what should I see but a number of buzzards hovering over my corn-field. 'The rascal has been there,' said I, 'for that sign is certain :' and, sure enough, on examining, I found the bones of what had been as beautiful a hog the day before, as was ever raised by a Buckeye. Then I tracked the critter out of the field to the woods, and all the marks he left behind, showed me that he was *the bear.*

"Well, stranger, the first fair chase I ever had with that big critter, I saw him no less than three distinct times at a distance : the dogs run him over eighteen miles and broke down, my horse gave out, and I was as nearly used up as a man can be, made on *my* principle, *which is patent.*

"Before this adventure, such things were unknown to me as possible; but, strange as it was, that bear got me used to it before I was done with him; for he got so at last, that he would leave me on a long chase *quite easy.* How he did it, I never could understand.

"That a bear runs at all, is puzzling; but how this one could tire down and bust up a pack of hounds and a horse, that were used to overhauling every thing they started after in no time, was past my understanding. Well, stranger, that bear finally got so sassy, that he used to help himself to a hog off my premises whenever he wanted one; the buzzards followed after what he left, and so, between *bear and buzzard*, I rather think I got *out of pork.*

" Well, missing that bear so often took hold of my vitals, and I wasted away. The thing had been carried too far, and it reduced me in flesh faster than an ager. I would see that bear in every thing I did : *he hunted me,* and that, too, like a devil, which I began to think he was.

" While in this shaky fix, I made preparations to give him a last brush, and be done with it. Having completed every thing to my satisfaction, I started at sunrise, and to my great joy, I discovered from the way the dogs run, that they were near him. Finding his trail was nothing, for that had become as plain to the pack as a turnpike road.

" On we went, and coming to an open country, what should I see but the bear very leisurely ascending a hill, and the dogs close at his heels, either a match for him this time in speed, or else he did not care to get out of their way—I don't know which. But wasn't he a beauty, though ! I loved him like a brother.

" On he went, until he came to a tree, the limbs of which formed a crotch about six feet from the ground.

Into this crotch he got and seated himself, the dogs yelling all around it; and there he sat eyeing them as quiet as a pond in low water.

"A greenhorn friend of mine, in company, reached shooting distance before me, and blazed away, hitting the critter in the centre of his forehead. The bear shook his head as the ball struck it, and then walked down from that tree, as gently as a lady would from a carriage.

"'Twas a beautiful sight to see him do that—he was in such a rage, that he seemed to be as little afraid of the dogs as if they had been sucking pigs; and the dogs warn't slow in making a ring around him at a respectful distance, I tell you; even Bowieknife himself, stood off. Then the way his eyes flashed!—why the fire of them would have singed a cat's hair; in fact, that bear was in a *wrath all over*. Only one pup came near him, and he was brushed out so totally with the bear's left paw, that he entirely disappeared; and that made the old dogs more cautious still. In the mean time, I came up, and taking deliberate aim, as a man should do, at his side, just back of his foreleg, *if my gun did not snap*, call me a coward, and I won't take it personal.

"Yes, stranger, *it snapped*, and I could not find a cap about my person. While in this predicament, I turned round to my fool friend—'Bill,' says I, 'you're an ass—you're a fool—you might as well have tried to kill that bear by barking the tree under his belly, as to

have done it by hitting him in the head. Your shot
has made a tiger of him; and blast me, if a dog gets
killed or wounded when they come to blows, I will stick
my knife into your liver, I will ———.' My wrath was up.
I had lost my caps, my gun had snapped, the fellow
with me had fired at the bear's head, and I expected
every moment to see him close in with the dogs and
kill a dozen of them at least. In this thing I was mistaken; for the bear leaped over the ring formed by the
dogs, and giving a fierce growl, was off—the pack, of
course, in full cry after him. The run this time was
short, for coming to the edge of a lake, the varmint
jumped in, and swam to a little island in the lake, which
it reached, just a moment before the dogs.

"'I'll have him now,' said I, for I had found my
caps in the *lining of my coat*—so, rolling a log into the
lake, I paddled myself across to the island, just as the
dogs had cornered the bear in a thicket. I rushed up
and fired—at the same time the critter leaped over the
dogs and came within three feet of me, running like
mad; he jumped into the lake, and tried to mount the
log I had just deserted, but every time he got half his
body on it, it would roll over and send him under; the
dogs, too, got around him, and pulled him about, and
finally Bowieknife clenched with him, and they sunk
into the lake together.

" Stranger, about this time I was excited, and I
stripped off my coat, drew my knife, and intended to

have taken a part with Bowieknife myself, when the bear rose to the surface. But the varmint staid under—Bowieknife came up alone, more dead than alive, and with the pack came ashore.

"'Thank God!' said I, 'the old villain has got his deserts at last.'

"Determined to have the body, I cut a grape-vine for a rope, and dove down where I could see the bear in the water, fastened my rope to his leg, and fished him, with great difficulty, ashore. Stranger, may I be chawed to death by young alligators, if the thing I looked at wasn't a *she bear, and not the old critter after all.*

"The way matters got mixed on that island was on-accountably curious, and thinking of it made me more than ever convinced that I was hunting the devil him-self. I went home that night and took to my bed—the thing was killing me. The entire team of Arkan-saw in bear-hunting acknowledged himself used up, and the fact sunk into my feelings as a snagged boat will in the Mississippi. I grew as cross as a bear with two cubs and a sore tail. The thing got out 'mong my neigh-bors, and I was asked how come on that individ-u-al that never lost a bear when once started? and if that same individ-u-al didn't wear telescopes when he turned a she-bear, of ordinary size, into an old he one, a little larger than a horse?

"'Prehaps,' said I, 'friends'—getting wrathy—'pre-haps you want to call somebody a liar?'

" ' Oh, no,' said they, ' we only heard of such things being *rather common* of late, but we don't believe one word of it; oh, no,'—and then they would ride off, and laugh like so many hyenas over a dead nigger.

It was too much, and I determined to catch that bear, go to Texas, or die,—and I made my preparations accordin'.

"I had the pack shut up and rested. I took my rifle to pieces, and iled it.

"I put caps in every pocket about my person, *for fear of the lining.*

"I then told my neighbors, that on Monday morning —naming the day—I would start THAT B(E)AR, and bring him home with me, or they might divide my settlement among them, the owner having disappeared.

" Well, stranger, on the morning previous to the great day of my hunting expedition, I went into the woods near my house, taking my gun and Bowieknife along, just *from habit*, and there sitting down, also from habit, what should I see, getting over my fence, but *the bear!* Yes, the old varmint was within a hundred yards of me, and the way he walked *over that fence*—stranger; he loomed up like a *black mist*, he seemed so large, and he walked right towards me.

"I raised myself, took deliberate aim, and fifed. Instantly the varmint wheeled, gave a yell, and *walked through the fence*, as easy as a failing tree would through a cobweb.

" I started after, but was tripped up by my inexpressibles, which, either from habit or the excitement of
the moment, were about my heels, and before I had
really gathered myself up, I heard the old varmint
groaning, like a thousand sinners, in a thicket near by,
and, by the time I reached him, he was a corpse.

"Stranger, it took five niggers and myself to put that
carcass on a mule's back, and old long-ears waddled
under his load, as if he was foundered in every leg of
his body; and with a common whopper of a bear, he
would have trotted off, and enjoyed himself.

" 'Twould astonish you to know how big he was:
I made a *bed-spread of his skin*, and the way it used
to cover my bear mattress, and leave several feet on each
side to tuck up, would have delighted you. It was, in
fact, a creation bear, and if it had lived in Samson's
time, and had met him in a fair fight, he would have
licked him in the twinkling of a dice-box.

"But, stranger, I never liked the way I hunted him,
and missed him. There is something curious about it,
that I never could understand,—and I never was satisfied at his giving in so *easy at last*. Prehaps he had
heard of my preparations to hunt him the next day, so
he jist guv up, like Captain Scott's coon, to save his
wind to grunt with in dying; but that ain't likely. My
private opinion is, that that bear was an *unhuntable bear*,
and died when his time come."

When this story was ended, our hero sat some min-

utes with his auditors, in a grave silence; I saw there
was a mystery to him connected with the bear whose
death he had just related, that had evidently made a
strong impression on his mind. It was also evident
that there was some superstitious awe connected with
the affair,—a feeling common with all "children of the
wood," when they meet with any thing out of their
every-day experience.

He was the first one, however, to break the silence,
and, jumping up, he asked all present to "liquor" before
going to bed,—a thing which he did, with a number of
companions, evidently to his heart's content.

Long before day, I was put ashore at my place of
destination, and I can only follow with the reader, in
imagination, our Arkansas friend, in his adventures at
the "Forks of Cypress," on the Mississippi.

THE MISSISSIPPI.

"I have been
Where the wild will of Mississippi's tide
Has dashed me on the sawyer."—BRAINERD.

THE North American continent—in its impenetrable forests—its fertile prairies—its magnificent lakes—its variety of rivers with their falls—is the richest portion of our globe. Many of these wonderful exhibitions of nature are already shrines, where pilgrims from every land assemble to admire and marvel at the surpassing wonders of a new world. So numerous indeed are the objects presented, so novel and striking is their character, that the judgment is confused in endeavoring to decide which single one is worthy of the greatest admiration; and the forests—the prairies—the lakes—the rivers—and falls—each in turn dispute the supremacy.

But to us, the Mississippi ranks first in importance; and thus we think must it strike all, when they consider the luxurious fertility of the valley through which it flows, its vast extent, and the charm of mystery that rests upon its waters.

The Niagara Falls, with its fearful depths, its rocky heights, its thunder, and " bows of promise," addresses itself to the ear, and the eye; and through these alone impresses the beholder with the greatness of its character. The Mississippi, on the contrary, although it may have few or no tangible demonstrations of power, although it has no language with which it can startle the senses, yet in a " still small voice " addresses the mind with its terrible lessons of strength and sublimity, more forcibly than any other object in nature.

The name MISSISSIPPI, was derived from the aborigines of the country, and has been poetically rendered the " Father of Waters." There is little truth in this translation, and it gives no idea, or scarcely none, of the river itself. The literal meaning of the Indian compound, Mississippi, as is the case with all Indian names in this country, would have been much better, and every way more characteristic. From the most numerous Indian tribe in the southwest we derive the name; and it would seem that the same people who gave the name to the Mississippi, at different times possessed nearly half the continent; judging from the fact that the Ohio in the north, and many of the most southern points of the peninsula of Florida, are named from the Choctaw language.

With that tribe the two simple adjectives, *Missah*

and *Sippah*, are used when describing the most familiar things ; but these two words, though they are employed thus familiarly, when separated—compounded, form the most characteristic name we can get of this wonderful river.   Missah, literally *Old big*, Sippah, *strong*, OLD-BIG-STRONG ; and this name is eminently appropriate to the Mississippi.

The country through which this river flows, is almost entirely alluvial.   Not a stone is to be seen, save about its head-waters ; and the dark rich earth "looks eager for the hand of cultivation ;" for vegetation lies piled upon its surface with a luxuriant wastefulness that beggars all description, and finds no comparison for its extent, except in the mighty river from which it receives its support.   This alluvial soil forms but frail banks wherewith to confine the swift current of the Mississippi ; and, as might be imagined, these are continually altering their shape and location.

The channel is capricious and wayward in its course. The needle of the compass turns round and round upon its axis, as it marks the bearings of your craft, and in a few hours will frequently point due north, west, east, and south, delineating those tremendous bends in the stream which nature seems to have formed to check the headlong current, and keep it from rushing too madly to the ocean.

But the stream does not always tamely circumscribe these bends : gathering strength from resistance, it will form new and more direct channels; and thus it is, that large tracts of country once upon the river, become inland, or are entirely swept away by the current; and so frequently does this happen, that " cut-offs " are almost as familiar to the eye on the Mississippi, as its muddy waters.

When the Mississippi, in making its "cut-offs," is ploughing its way through the virgin soil, there float upon the top of this destroying tide, thousands of trees, which but lately covered the land, and lined its caving banks. These gigantic wrecks of the primitive forests are tossed about by the invisible power of the current, as if they were straws; and they find no rest, until with associated thousands they are thrown upon some projecting point of land, where they lie rotting for miles, their dark forms frequently shooting into the air like writhing serpents, presenting one of the most desolate pictures of which the mind can conceive. These masses of timber are called " rafts."

Other trees become attached to the bottom of the river, and yet by some elasticity of the roots are loose enough to be affected by the strange and powerful current, which will bear them down under the surface; and the trees, by their own strength, will come gracefully up again to be again ingulfed; and thus they continuously wave upward and downward, with a gracefulness of motion which would not disgrace a beau of the old school. Boats frequently pass over these " sawyers," as they go down

5

stream, pressing them under by their weight; but let some unfortunate child of the genius of Robert Fulton, as it passes up stream, be saluted by the visage of one of these polite gentry, as it rises ten or more feet in the air, and nothing short of irreparable damage, or swift destruction ensues : while the cause of all this disaster, after the concussion, will rise above the ruin as if nothing had happened, shake the dripping water from its forked limbs, and sink and rise again, rejoicing in its strength.

Other trees become firmly fastened in the bed of the river; and their long trunks, shorn of their limbs, present the most formidable objects of navigation. A rock itself, sharpened and set by art, could be no more dangerous than these dread " snags." Let the bows of the strongest vessel come in contact with them, and the concussion will crush its timbers as if they were paper; and the noble craft will tremble for a moment like a thing of life, when suddenly stricken to its vitals, and then sink into its grave.

Such are the " cut-offs," " rafts," " sawyers," and " snags," of the Mississippi; terms significant to the minds of the western boatman and hunter, of qualities which they apply to themselves, and to their heroes, whenever they wish to express themselves strongly; and we presume that the beau-ideal of a political character with them, would be, one who would come at the truth by a " cut-off "—separate and pile up falsehood for de-

cay like the trees of a " raft : " and do all this with the
politeness of a " sawyer"—and with principles unyield-
ing as a " snag."

The forests that line the banks of the Mississippi,
and supply, without any apparent decrease, the vast
masses of timber that in such varied combinations
every where meet the eye, are themselves worthy of the
river which they adorn.

Go into the primitive forests at noonday, and however fiercely the sun may shine, you will find yourself
enveloped in gloom. Gigantic trees obstruct your pathway, and as you cast your eyes upward, your head grows
dizzy with their height. Here, too, are to be seen dead
trunks, shorn of their limbs, and whitening in the blasts,
that are as mighty in their size as the pillars of Hercu-
les. Grape-vines larger than your body will, for some
distance, creep along the ground, and then suddenly
spring a hundred feet into the air, grasp some patriarch
of the forest in its folds, crush, mutilate, and destroy it;
and then, as if to make amends for the injury, throw over
its deadening work the brightest green, the richest foliage, filled with fragrance, and the clustering grape.
On the top of these aspiring trees, the squirrel is beyond
the gunshot reach of the hunter.

Upon the ground are long piles of crumbling mould,
distinguished from the earth around them by their numerous and variegated flowers. These immense piles,
higher in places than your head, are but the remains of

single trees, that a century ago startled the silence now
so profound, and with their headlong crash sent through
the green arch above sounds that for a moment silenced
the echoing thunder that loaded the hurricane that pros
trated them.

Here were to be seen the ruins of a new continent—
here were mouldering the antiquities of America—how unlike those of the Old World. Omnipotence, not man, had
created these wonderful monuments of greatness, with no
other tears than the silent rain, no other slavery than
the beautiful laws that govern nature in ordering the
seasons—and yet these monuments, created in inno-
cency, and at the expense of so much time, were wasting
into nothingness. God above in his power could erect
them. They were breathed upon in anger and turned to
dust.

The vast extent of the Mississippi is almost beyond
belief. The stream which may bear you gently along in
midwinter, so far south that the sun is oppressive, finds
its beginnings in a country of eternal snows. Follow it
in your imagination thousands of miles, as you pass on
from its head waters to its mouth, and you find it flowing through almost every climate under heaven : nay
more—the comparatively small stream on which you
look, receives within itself the waters of four rivers
alone ; Arkansas, Red, Ohio, and Missouri ; whose
united length, without including their tributaries, is
over eight thousand miles. Yet, this mighty flood is

swallowed up by the Mississippi, as if it possessed within itself the very capacity of the ocean, and disdained in its comprehensive limits, to acknowledge the accession of strength.

The color of this tremendous flood of water is always turbid. There seems no rest for it, that will enable it to become quiet or clear. In all seasons the same muddy water meets the eye; and this strange peculiarity suggests to the mind that the banks of the river itself are composed of this dark sediment which has in the course of centuries confined the onward flood within its present channel, and in this order of nature we find one of the most original features of the river; for on the Mississippi we have no land sloping in gentle declivities to the water's edge, but a bank just high enough, where it is washed by the river, to protect the back country from inundation, in the ordinary rises of the stream; for whenever, from an extensive flood, it rises above the top of this feeble barrier, the water runs down into the country.

This singular fact shows how all the land on the Mississippi south of the thirty-fourth degree of latitude, is liable to inundation, since nearly all the inhabitants on the shores of the river, find its level, in ordinarily high water, running above the land on which they reside. To prevent this easy, and apparently natural inundation, there seems to be a power constantly exerted to hold the flood in check, and bid it "go so far and no farther ;" and but for this interposition of Divine power, here so signally displayed, the fair fields of the South would become mere sand-bars upon the shores of the Atlantic, and the country which might now support the world by its luxurious vegetation, would only bear the angry ocean wave.

Suppose, for an instant, that a universal spring should beam upon our favored continent, and that the thousands of streams which are tributary to the Mississippi were to become at once unloosed: the mighty flood in its rushing course would destroy the heart of the northwestern continent.

But mark the goodness and wisdom of Providence ! Early in the spring, the waters of the Ohio rise with its tributaries, and the Mississippi bears them off without injuriously overflowing its banks. When summer sets in, its own head-waters about the lakes, and the swift Missouri, with its melting ice from the Rocky Mountains, come down ; and thus each, in order, makes the Mississippi its outlet to the Gulf of Mexico. But were all these streams permitted to come together in their strength, what, again we ask, would save the Eden gardens of the South ?

In contemplations like these, carried out to their fullest extent, we may arrive at the character of this mighty river. *It is in the thoughts it suggests*, and not in the breadth or length visible at any given point to the eye. Depending on the senses alone, we should never be confounded by astonishment, or excited by admiration. You may float upon its bosom, and be lost amid its world of waters, and yet *see* nothing of its vastness; for the river has no striking beauty; its waves run scarce as high as a child can reach; upon its banks we find no towering precipices, no cloud-capped mountains—all, all is dull,—a dreary waste.

Let us float however, day after day, upon its apparently sluggish surface, and by comparison once begin to comprehend its magnitude, and the mind becomes overwhelmed with fearful admiration. There seems to rise up from its muddy waters a spirit robed in mystery, that points back for its beginning to the deluge, and whispers audibly, " I roll on, and on, and on, *altering*, but *not altered*, while time exists! "

Here, too, we behold a power terrible in its loneliness; for on the Mississippi a sameness meets your eye every where, with scarce a single change of scene.

A river incomprehensible, illimitable, and mysterious, flows ever onward, tossing to and fro under its depths, in its own channel, as if fretting in its ordered limits; swallowing its banks here, and disgorging them elsewhere, so suddenly that the attentive pilot, as he repeats his frequent route, feels that he knows not where he is, and often hesitates fearfully along in the mighty flood, guided only by the certain lead; and again and again is he startled by the ominous cry, " Less fathom deep! "

where but yesterday the lead would have in vain gone down for soundings.

Such is the great Aorta of the continent of North America; alone and unequalled in its majesty, it proclaims in its course the wisdom and power of GOD, who only can measure its depths, and " turn them about as a very little thing."

LARGE AND SMALL STEAMERS OF THE MISSISSIPPI.

THE steamboats of the Mississippi are as remarkable for size and form as the river itself. Gigantic specimens of art that go bellowing over the swift and muddy current, like restless monsters, breathing out the whisperings of the hurricane, clanking and groaning as if an earthquake was preparing to convulse the world, obscuring in clouds of smoke the sun in the daytime, or rolling over the darkness of night a flame as if the volcano had burst from the bosom of the deep.

Who, without wondering, sees them for the first time, as they rush along, filled with an ever-busy throng of travellers, and loaded with the boundless wealth, that teems from the rich soil, as the reward of the labor of the American husbandman!

The Mississippi is also very remarkable for little steamboats, small specimens of water-craft, that are

5*

famous ror their ambitious puffings, noisy captains, and gigantic placards—boats that run up little streams that empty into the Mississippi—boats that go beyond places never dreamed of in geography—never visited by travellers, or even marked down in the scrutinizing book of the tax collector.

The first time one finds himself in one of these boats, he looks about him as did Gulliver when he got in Lilliput. It seems as if you are larger and more magnificent than an animated colossus—you find, on going on the boat, that your feet are on the lower deck and your head up-stairs; the after-cabin is so disposed of that you can sit inside of it, and yet be near the bows. The ladies' cabin has but one berth in it, and that only as wide as a shelf.

The machinery is tremendous; two large kettles firmly set in brick, attached to a complicated-looking coffee mill, two little steampipes and one big one.

And then the way that the big steam-pipe will smoke, and the little ones let off steam, is singular. Then the puffing of the little coffee-mill! why it works as spitefully as a tom-cat with his tail caught in the crack of a door.

Then the engineer, to see him open "the furnace" doors, and pitch in wood, and open the little stop-cocks to see if the steam is not too high, all so much like a big steamer. Then the name of the craft, " THE U. S. MAIL, EMPEROR," the letters covering over the whole side of the boat, so that it looks like a locomotive advertisement.

Then the " u. s. mail " deposited in one corner of the cabin, and two rifles standing near, as if to guard it; said mail being in a bag that looks like a gigantic shot-pouch, fastened to a padlock, and said pouch filled with three political speeches, franked by M. C.'s, one letter, to a man who did not live at the place of its destination, and a small bundle of post-office documents put in by mistake.

The bell that rang for the boat's departure, was a tremendous bell; it swung to and fro awfully; it was big enough for a cathedral, and as it rung for the twentieth, 'last time,' one passenger came on board weighing about three hundred, and the boat got under way.

" Let go that hawser," shouted the captain in a voice of thunder. *Pe, wee, wee, pish*, went the little steampipe, and we were off. Our track lay for a time down the Mississippi, and we went ahead furiously, overhauled two rafts and a flat-boat within two hours, and presented the appearance of a real big steamer most valiantly, by nearly shaking to pieces in its waves. The two light passengers got along very well, but whenever the fat passenger got off a line with the centre of the cabin, the pilot would give the bell one tap, and the captain would bawl out, " Trim the boat."

Captain Raft, of the U. S. Mail steamer Emperor, it may not be uninteresting to know, was one of those eccentric men that had a singular ambition to run a boat where no one else could—he was fond of being a great discoverer on a small scale.   In one of his eccentric humors, Captain Raft run the Emperor up Red River, as the pilot observed, about " a feet," which in the southwest, means several hundred miles.

Among the passengers upon that occasion was old Zeb Marston, a regular out-and-outer frontiersman, who seemed to spend his whole life in settling out of the way places, and locating his family in sickly situations.   Zeb was the first man that " blazed " a tree in Eagle Town, on the Mountain Fork, and he was the first man that ever choked an alligator to death with his hands, on the Big Cossitot.   He knew every snag, sawyer, nook and corner of the Sabine, the Upper Red River, and their tributaries, and when "bar whar scace," he was wont to declare war on the Cumanchos, and, for excitement, " used them up terribly."

But to our story—Zeb moved on Red River, settled in a low, swampy, terrible place, and he took it as a great honor that the Emperor passed his cabin ; and, at every trip the boat made, there was tumbled out at Zeb's yard a barrel of new whiskey, (as regularly as she passed,) for which was paid the full value in cord wood.

Now, Captain Raft was a kind man, and felt disposed to oblige every resident that lived on his route of travel; but it was unprofitable to get every week to Zeb's out-of-the-way place, and as he landed the fifteenth barrel,

he expressed his surprise at the amount of whiskey consumed at his " settlement," and hinted it was rather an
unprofitable business for the boat. Zeb, at this piece
of information, " flared up," raised his mane, shut his
" maulers," and told Captain Raft he could whip him,—
the pilot, and deck hands, and if they would give him
the advantage of the " under grip," he would let the pis-
ton-rod of the engine punch him in the side all the time
the fight was going on.

Raft, at this display of fury from Zeb, cooled down
immediately, acknowledged himself " snagged," begged
Zeb's pardon, and adjourned to the bar for a drink.
One glass followed another, until the heroes got into
the mellow mood, and Zeb, on such occasions, always
" went it strong " for his family. After praising their
beauty individually and collectively, he broke into the
pathetic, and set the Captain crying, by the following
heart-rending appeal :—

" Raft, Raft, my dear fellow, you talk about the
trouble of putting out a barrel of whiskey every week
at my diggins, when I have got a sick wife, and five small
children, and *no cow !*—whar's your heart ? "

Dinner in due course of time was announced—the
table was covered with the largest roast beef, the largest
potatoes, and the largest carving-knife and fork that
ever floated, and the steward rang the largest bell for
dinner, and longer than any other steward would have
done, and the captain talked about the immense extent

of the Mississippi, the contemplated canal through the Isthmus of Darien, and the ability of the steam war-ships; he said, that in the contemplation of the subject, "his feelings war propelled by five hundred horse-power—that the bows of his imagination cut through the muddy waters of reality—that the practicability of his notions was as certain as a rudder in giving the proper direction—that his judgment, like a safety-valve to his mind, would always keep him from advocating any thing that would burst up, and that it was unfortunate that Robert Fulton had not lived to be President of the United States."

With such enlarged ideas he wiled away the hours of dinner;—arriving at the mouth of "Dry Outlet" (a little ditch that draws off some of the waters of the Mississippi when very high), the pilot turned the bows of the "Emperor" into its mouth, and shot down, along with an empty flour barrel, with an alacrity that sent the bows of the boat high and dry on land, the first bend it came to.

A great deal of hard work got it off, and away the steamer went again, at one time sideways, at another every way, hitting against the soft alluvial banks, or brushing the pipes among the branches of overhanging trees. Finally the current got too strong, and carried it along with alarming velocity. The bows of the boat were turned up stream, and thus managed to keep an onward progress compatible with safety.

The banks of the "dry outlet" were very low and very swampy, and were disfigured occasionally by wretched cabins, in which lived human beings, who, the captain of the "Emperor" informed us, lived, as far as he could judge, by sitting upon the head of a barrel and looking out on the landscape, and at his boat as it passed. From the fact that they had no arable land, and looked like creatures fed on unhealthy air, we presume that was their only occupation.

In time we arrived at the "small village," the destination of the "mail pouch;" "the passengers" landed and visited the town. It was one of the ruins of a great city, dreamed of by land speculators in "glorious times." Several splendidly-conceived mansions were decaying about in the half-finished frames that were strewn upon the ground. A barrel of whiskey was rolled ashore, the mail delivered, the fat man got out, and the steamer was again under way.

The "dry outlet" immerged into a broad inland lake, which itself, with a peculiarity of the tributaries of the Mississippi, emptied into that river. Our little boat plunged on, keeping up with untiring consistency all its original pretensions and puffing, and the same clanking of tiny machinery, scaring the wild ducks and geese, scattering the white cranes over our heads, and making the cormorant screech with astonishment in hoarser tones than the engine itself.

Occasionally we would land at a " squatter's settlement," turn round and come up to the banks with grandeur, astonishing the squatter's children, and the invalid hens that lived in the front yard. The captain would pay up the bill for the wood, and off he would go again as " big as all out doors," and a great deal more natural. Thus we struggled on, until, sailing up a stream with incessant labor, such as we went down when we commenced our sketch, we emerged into the world of water that flows in the Mississippi. Down the rapid current we gracefully swept, very much to the astonishment of the permanent inhabitants on its banks.

Again for the " innumerable time," the " furnaces " consumed the wood, and as it had to be replenished, we ran alongside one of those immense wood-yards, so peculiar to the Mississippi, where lay, in one continuous pile, thousands of cords of wood. The captain of the " Emperor," as he stopped his boat before it, hollowed out from his upper deck, in a voice of the loudest tone— " Got any wood here ? "

Now the owner of the wood-yard, who was a very rich man, and a very surly one, looked on the "pile," and said " he *thought it possible.*"

" Then," said the captain, " how do you sell it a cord ? "

The woodman eyed the boat and its crew; and eyed the passengers, and then said, " he would not sell the boat any wood, but the crew might come ashore and *get their hats full of chips for nothing.*"

Hereupon the five hundred horse-power of the captain's feelings, and the rudder and the safety-valves of his well-regulated mind, became surcharged with wrath, and he vented out abuse on the wood-yard and its owner, which was expressed in " thoughts that breathe and words that burn."

A distant large boat, breasting the current like a thing of life, at this moment coming in sight, gave us a hint, and rushing ashore amid the " wrath," we bid the " Emperor " and its enraged captain a hearty good-bye, and in a few moments more we dwindled into insignificance on board of the magnificent ———, the pride and wonder of the Western waters.

FAMILIAR SCENES ON THE MISSISSIPPI.

As our magnificent Union has increased in population, the aborigines within the " older States " have become constantly more and more degraded. " The Government," as the most merciful policy, has taxed its energies to remove these red men from the vicinity of civilization, to homes still wild and primitive, west of the Mississippi. There, a vast extent of country is still unoccupied, in which he can pursue, comparatively unrestrained, his inclinations, and pluck a few more days of happiness before his sun entirely sets.

Occasionally may be seen in the southwest, a large body of these people, under the charge of a " government officer," going to the new homes provided for them by their " white father." These " removals " are always melancholy exhibitions. The Indians, dispirited and heart-broken, entirely hopeless of the future, with dogged looks submit to every privation that is imposed on them, and appear equally indifferent as to the receipt of favors.   Throwing aside every mark of etiquette among themselves, the chief, who, when among their native haunts, is almost a sacred person, lies down or takes his food, promiscuously with the noblest or most degraded of his people ; all distinctions of age as well as caste, are thrown aside, and the Indians seem a mere mass of degraded humanity, with less apparent capability of self-preservation than the brute.

Some two or three years ago, we took passage on board a boat bound from New Orleans to St. Louis, which boat the government had engaged to carry as far towards their place of destination as practicable, near four hundred Seminoles, who, with their chiefs, had agreed to emigrate west of the Mississippi.

We were not particularly pleased with our numerous and novel passengers, but the lateness of the season lessened the chances of getting a conveyance, and as most of the Indians were to remain in a tender, lashed to the side of the steamer, we concluded that a study of their manners and habits would beguile away the time of a long trip, and thus pay us for the inconveniences we might be put to.   Unfortunately, the novelty of our situation too soon passed away.

The Indians, who on first acquaintance kept up a little display of their original character, gradually relapsed into what appeared to be a mere vegetable existence, and slept through the entire twenty-four hours of the day. Of all the remarkable traits of character that dignify them in history, we could not discern the least trace; yet among the brutal, insensible savages at our feet, were many daring spirits, who had displayed in their warfare with the whites, dangerous talents, and taken many a bloody scalp. The girls were possessed of little or no personal charms, while the women, the laborers of the tribe, were as hideous as any hags that can be imagined.

The heat of the weather and the confinement of the boat, had a dreadful effect upon these poor wretches; sickness rapidly broke out among them, and as they stoutly refused to take the white man's medicine, their chances of recovery were poor indeed.

The tender was turned into a perfect lazar-house, and nothing could be seen but the affecting attentions of the old squaws to their friends and relatives, as they wasted away before their eyes. The infant and patriarch were side by side, consuming with slow fever, while the corpse of some middle-aged person lay at their feet, waiting for the funeral rites and the obscurity of the grave. Vain were the prescriptions of the " medicine man " of their tribe; he blew his breath through a gaudy colored reed upon the faces of his patients, and recited his incantations, but without success. He disfigured his person with new paint, and altered his devices daily, still his patients would die, and at every landing where the boat stopped, some poor Indian was taken ashore and hastily buried.

No one mourned over the corpse but the females, and they only when intimately related to the deceased. The father, son, or husband, as they saw their relatives falling around them, scarce turned their eyes upon the dead, and if they did, it was only to exclaim in guttural 'accents, " Ugh ! " and then turn away to sleep.

Not an article belonging to the dead but was wrapped up with it, or placed in the coffin; the infant and its playthings, the young girl and her presents, the squaw with her domestic utensils, and the " brave " with his gun and whatever property there was in his possession. A beautiful custom, indeed—and one that brings no crocodile tears to the eyes of the living heir, and gives the lawyer no chance for litigation.

Among those who died, was one old veteran warrior who had particularly attracted our attention by his severe looks and. loneliness of habit, and we watched attentively his. exit from the world. He seemed, as near as we could judge, to have no relatives about him; no one noticed him but the doctor, who was markedly attentive. The old man was a chief, and the scars that covered his body told of many a dreadful encounter with man and beast. His huge skeleton, as he moved about in his ill-concealed agony, looked like the remains of a giant, exaggerated by its want of flesh. His hands were small, and of feminine delicacy—occasionally he would move them about in mute eloquence, then clutch at the air, as if in pursuit of an enemy, and fall back exhausted.

Recovering from one of these fits, he tried to stand, but found it impossible; he, however, raised himself upon his elbow, and opening his eyes for the first time in a long while, stared wildly about him. The sun, which was at this time low in the west, shone full upon him— his smooth skin glistened like burnished copper—his long-neglected hair, of silvery whiteness, hung over his head and face, while the scalp-lock displayed itself by its immense length, as it reached his shoulder. His muscles, shrunken by age and disease, moved like cords in performing their offices.

A smile lit up his features—his lips moved—and he essayed to speak. A faint chant was heard—the doctor, at the sound, bent his head, and assumed an air of reverence. The chant, as it continued to swell on the evening breeze, reached the ears of the slumbering warriors that lay about, and as they listened to the sounds, I could discern their sottish eyes open and flash with unearthly fires; sometimes exhibiting pleasure, but oftener ferocity and hatred. The old man sang on, a few raised to their feet, and waved their hands in the air, as if keeping time, and occasionally some aged Indian would repeat the sounds he heard. The old man ceased, turned his face full to the setting sun, and fell back a corpse.

The Indians cast a look in the direction of their

homes, gave an expression of malignity, as well as sorrow, and then silently and sluggishly sank into repose, as if nothing unusual had occurred.

"That old fellow brags well of his infernal deeds," observed one of the white men accompanying the Indians, "and the red-skinned devils about here drink it in as a Cuba hound would blood."

The intense heat of the weather, and the quietness that reigned so profoundly among the Indians, broken only by the saw and hammer of the carpenter making coffins at the capstan, made us sigh for a landing-place, and a separation from such melancholy scenes. This desire was encouraged from the well-known fact, that the savages grew every hour more troublesome, and the song of the dying old chief had neither allayed their feelings, nor made them more contented.

*   *   .   *   *   *

The morning following the death of the old chief had been preceded by one of those nights in which the fog rose from the water so thick, that, in the hyperbolical language of the boatman, you could make featherbeds of it. The pilot had "felt his way along" for many hours, until the sudden crash that shook every thing in the boat, convinced us that we were aground. The engine stopped, and left us in perfect silence and obscurity.

Long after our accustomed hour of rising, we went

on deck. The fresh mist blew in our faces with sickening effect, and the sun—then two hours high—was invisible. The shore, which was so near that the breaking of twigs could be heard, as cattle, or game moved about on it, was indiscernible. Even the end of the boat opposite to the one on which we stood was invisible. A deep, damp, opaque Mississippi river fog, had swallowed us up.

As the sun continued to rise and gain strength in its ascent, its rays penetrated through the gloom, and we at last discovered it, working its way through the fog by its rays, reaching them out as a debilitated spider would his legs, and apparently with the same caution and labor.

With the growing heat a gentle breeze sprang up, and the fog rolled about in huge masses, leaving spots of pure atmosphere, and then closing them up; gradually the air became more and more rarefied, and things at a distance began to appear all magnified and mysterious.

On came the sun, brightening and enlarging, until his streaming rays dipped into the water, and shot up to the zenith.

The fog, no longer able to keep its consistency, retired before its splendor in little clouds, which would sometimes rally, and spread over the surface of the river, then, breaking asunder, vanish away into air, with a splendor that rivalled the dying dolphin's tints.

Now, for the first time, could we learn our where-abouts. The broad bosom of the Mississippi stretched far to the front of us, while at the stern of our boat was one of those abrupt banks that denote a sudden bend in the river. This had deceived the pilot. On our right, within a few hundred yards, lay the shore, lined with huge trees, tangled with gigantic vines, and waving with festoons of moss, giving them a sombre appearance, that was singular and repulsive. Wild ducks and geese went screaming by, heron and crane innumerable would come near us, but discovering the dark form of our boat, fly precipitately away.

The water glistened in the sun, and there would rise from its quiet surface little columns of mist, that would ascend high in the air, or sail along on the surface of the water, until striking the distant shore, they rolled over the landscape, enveloping parts in momentary ob-scurity,—and it was not until near noon that the fog entirely disappeared. Then the sun, as if incensed with the veil that had for a time kept it from its scorching work, poured down its heat with more intensity, leaving a foggy day, hotter before its close, than if the sun had been unobscured in its appearance in the morn.

While sitting in the cabin, congratulating ourselves on the prospect of getting off the sand-bar, on which we had so long been detained, the report of a rifle was heard, fired from the deck, accompanied by a yell.

Another rifle was discharged, and a loud Indian

whoop followed, that made our blood run cold.   The ladies present turned pale, and the commanding officer
who had charge of the Indians, somewhat astonished, left
the cabin.

A momentary alarm seized upon us all.   Could the
old warrior's death-song have incited mutiny !—Crack !
went another rifle outside,—and another shout ;—we
could stand it no longer, but rushed on deck.

What a scene !   Not an Indian that was able, but
was upon his feet, his eyes sparkling with fire, and his
form looking as active as a panther's.   The sluggards
of yesterday were sleek and nervous as horses at the
starting post, so perfectly had a little excitement altered
them.   Their rifles, however, thank Heaven, were not
turned upon the white man—their enemy was between
the boat and the shore—in the water—in the form of a
very large black bear.

It was a beautiful sight to see the savage springing
with a graceful bound, on some high place in the boat ;
and raise his rifle to his eye, ;—before the report was
heard you could mark a red furrow on the head of the
bear, where it was struck by the ball as it passed its
way through the skin and flesh without entering the
bone, while the bear, at these assaults, would throw himself half out of the water, brush over the smarting
wound with his huge paw, and then dash on for life.
Another shot, and another yell brought the bear on the
defensive, and showed that he was dangerously wounded.

While this firing was going on, some Indians, armed only with knives, launched a canoe that lay among their movables, and paddled hurriedly out to the bear. No sooner was the canoe within the bear's reach than he put his huge paws on its side, and in spite of the thrusts aimed at his head, turned his enemies with a somerset into the water. Loud shouts of laughter greeted this accident; the little " papooses " and women fairly danced with joy, while the crew yelled and shouted at the sport, as much as the savages themselves.

The bear turned from the boat and looked for his victims, but they were not to be seen; precipitated so suddenly into the water, they sank below the surface like the duck when much alarmed, and then thrust out their shining polls far from the friendly hug of the bear.

Laying their plans of attack at once (for the firing of rifles was suspended), one of the Indians attracted the bear's attention, and made towards him; they met, the floating canoe only between them, and while thus skirmishing, an unoccupied Indian came up behind the bear, raised his knife, and drove it deeply into his side, and then disappeared beneath the surface. The bear turned in the direction of this new attack, snapped and clawed in the water in the greatest agony. Another stab was given in the same way, and as the Indian again disappeared, a " white hunter," who had been heretofore an uninterested spectator, sprang upon the guards of the boat, and singing out "red devils, look out below," fired. The bear leaped entirely out of the water, fell upon his back, and after a convulsive kick or two, float-ed lifelessly upon the water.

This exploit of the white man, so sudden and unex-pected, was greeted by a loud shout from all parties.

'You see," said the hunter, as he coolly laid down his rifle—" you see the bear has a feeling, strangers, and whar is the use in tormenting the varmint? my old shooting iron never misses, but if it had hit a red-skin by accident, I should not have been ashamed of the shot —for the bear is the best Christian of the two, and a parfect gentleman, compared with the best copper-skin that ever breathed."

The Indians in the water at the last shot expressed a significant " ugh," and approaching the bear, gave him repeated thrusts with their knives, which showed that they thought him a hard-lived and dangerous animal. In a few minutes they recovered their canoe, and were towing the dead carcass ashore.

Fifty Indians at least now threw their blankets aside, and leaping into the water, swam after the bear. The tearing off of the huge skin, and jerking the meat, was dispatched so rapidly, that it indicated an accustomed work.

This little incident relieved the monotony, of all others the most disagreeable—that of being aground in the Mississippi, and the hours of labor which were spent in releasing the boat, passed quickly away, and by the time the Indians returned to their friends in the tender, the bell sounded;—we moved :—and the steamer again gallantly bore us toward our place of destination.

A STORM SCENE ON THE MISSISSIPPI.

In the year 18—, we found ourselves travelling on horse-back, "low down on the Mississippi." The weather was intensely hot, and as we threaded our way through the forests and swamps, through which the river flows, a silent and stifled atmosphere prevailed, such as required little wisdom to predict as the forerunner of a storm.

The insects of the woods were more than usually troublesome and venomous. The locust would occasion-ally make its shrill sounds as on a merry day, then sud-denly stop, give a disquiet chirp or two, and relapse into silence. The venomous mosquito, revelled in the damp-ness of the air, and suspending its clamor of distant trumpets, seemed only intent to bite. The crows scold-ed like unquiet housewives, high in the air, while higher still the buzzard wheeled in graceful but narrowed circles.

The dried twigs in our path bent, instead of snap-ping, as the weight of our horses' hoofs pressed upon them, while the animal would put forward his ears, as if expecting soon to be very much alarmed; and lastly, to make all those signs certain, the rheumatic limbs of an old Indian guide, who accompanied us, suddenly grew lame, for he went limping upon his delicately formed feet, and occasionally looking aloft with suspicious eyes, he proclaimed, that there would be "storm too much!"

A storm in the forest is no trifling affair; the tree under which you shelter yourself may draw the lightning upon your head, or its ponderous limbs, pressed upon by the winds, drag the heavy trunk to the earth, crushing you with itself in its fall; or some dead branch that has for years protruded from among the green foliage, may on the very occasion of your presence, fall to the ground and destroy you.

The rain too, which in the forest finds difficulty in soaking into the earth, will in a few hours fill up the ravines and water-courses, wash away the trail you may be following, or destroy the road over which you journey.

All these things we were from experience aware of, and as we were some distance from our journey's end, and also from any "settlement," we pressed forward to a "clearing," which was in our path, as a temporary stopping-place, until the coming storm should have passed away.

Our resting-place for the night was on the banks of the Mississippi; it consisted of a rude cabin in the centre of a small garden-spot and field, and had once been the residence of a squatter—but now deserted for causes unknown to us. The cabin was most pleasantly situated, and commanded a fine view of the river both up and down its channel.

We reached this rude dwelling just as the sun was setting, and his disappearance behind the lowlands of the Mississippi, was indeed glorious. Refracted by the humidity of the atmosphere into a vast globe of fire, it seemed to be kindling up the Cypress trees that stretched out before us, into a light blaze, while the gathering clouds extended the conflagration far north and south, and carried it upwards into the heavens. Indeed, so glorious for a moment was the sight, that we almost fancied that another Phæton was driving the chariot of the Sun, and that in its ungoverned course, its wheels were fired; and the illusion was quite complete, when we heard the distant thunder echoing from those brilliant clouds, and saw the lightning, like silver arrows, flash across the crimson heavens.

A moment more, and the sun was extinguished in the waters—all light disappeared, and the sudden darkness that follows sunset as you approach the tropics, was upon us.

With the delightful consciousness of having already escaped the storm, we gathered round a pleasant blaze formed of dried twigs, kindled by flashing powder in the pan of an old-fashioned gun. In the meantime, the thunder grew more and more distinct, the lightning flashed more brightly, and an occasional gust of wind, accompanied by sleet, would penetrate between the logs that composed our shelter.

An old wood-chopper, who made one of our party, feeling unusually comfortable, grew loquacious; and he detailed with great effect the woeful scenes he had been in at different times of his life, the most awful of which had been preceded, he said, by just such signs of weather as were then exhibiting themselves.

Among other adventures, he had been wrecked while acting as a "hand" on a flat-boat navigating the Mississippi.

He said he had come all the way from Pittsburgh, at the head of the Ohio, to within two or three hundred miles of Orleans, without meeting with any other serious accident, than that of getting out of whiskey twice.

But one night the captain of the flat-boat said that the weather was "crafty," a thing he thought himself, as it was most too quiet to last long.

After detailing several other particulars, he finished his story of being wrecked, as follows: "The quiet weather I spoke of, was followed by a sudden change; the river grew as rough as an alligator's back; thar was the tallest kind of a noise overhead, and the fire flew about up thar, like fur in a cat-fight.

" 'We'll put in shore,' said the captain; and we tried to do it, that's sartain; but the way in which we always

6*

walked off from a tree, whar we might have tied up, was a caution to steamboats.

"'Keep the current,' said the captain, 'and let us sweat it out.' We went on this way some time, when I told the captain—said I, Captain, I have never been in these diggins afore, but if I haven't seen the same landscape three times, then I can't speak the truth.

"At this the captain looked hard, and swore that we were in an eddy, and doing nothing but whirling round.

"The lightning just at this time was very accommodating, and showed us a big tree in the river that had stuck fast, and was bowing up and down, ready to receive us, and we found ourselves rushing straight on to it.

"The owner of the bacon and other 'plunder,' with which the boat was loaded, was on board,—and when he saw the 'sawyer,' he eyed it as hard as a small thief would a constable; says he, 'Captain, if that ar fellow at the sweep (oar) (fellow meant me)' said he 'Captain, if that ar fellow at the sweep don't bear on harder, and keep us off that tree, I am a busted-up pork merchant.' I did bear on it as well as I could, but the current was too strong, and we went on the 'sawyer' all standing. The boat broke up like a dried leaf; pork and plunder scattered, and I swam, half dead, to the shore.

"I lost in the whole operation just two shirts, eighteen dollars in wages, and half a box of Kaintucky tobacker, besides two game cocks.

" I tell you what, stranger, a storm on that ar Mississipp ain't to be sneezed at."

The wood-chopper's story, when concluded, would have occasioned a general laugh, had there not been outside our cabin at this moment a portentous silence, which alarmed us all.

The storm we thought had been upon us in all its fury, but we now felt that more was to come; in the midst of this expectation a stream of fire rushed from the horizon upwards; where high over head could be seen its zigzag course, then rushed downwards, apparently almost at our very feet,—a few hundred yards from us a tall oak dropped some of its gigantic limbs, and flashed into a light blaze. The rain, however powerful previously, now descended in one continued sheet. The roof of our shelter seemed to gather water rather than to protect us from it; little rivulets dashed across the floor, and then widening into streams, we were soon literally afloat. The descending floods sounded about us like the roll-call of a muffled drum, the noise almost deafening us, then dying off in the distance, as the sweeping gusts of wind drove the clouds before them. The burning forest meanwhile hissed and cracked, and rolled up great columns of steam.

The turbid water of the Mississippi in all this war of the elements, rushed on, save where it touched its banks, with a smooth but mysterious looking surface that resembled in the glare of the lightning, a mirror of bronze, and to heighten this almost unearthly effect, the forest trees that lined its most distant shores, rose up like mountains of impenetrable darkness, against clouds burning with fire.

The thunder cracked and echoed through the heavens, and the half starved wolf, nearly dead with fear, mingled his cries of distress with the noises without, startling us with the momentary conviction, that we heard the voices of men in the agony of death.

Hours passed away and the elements spent their fury; and although the rain continued falling in torrents, it was finally unaccompanied with lightning. So sudden, indeed, were the extremes, that with your eyes dilating with the glare of the heavens, you were, a moment after, surrounded by the most perfect darkness.

Confused, bewildered, and soaking wet; we followed the stoical example of our Indian guide, and settling down in a crouching attitude, waited most impatiently for the light of the morning.

The rain continued to descend in gusts, and the same deep darkness was upon us; my companions soon fell asleep as soundly as if they were at home; the long drawn respirations added to my misery. Wound up to the highest pitch of impatience, I was about starting to my feet to utter some angry complaint, when the Indian, whom I thought in a profound slumber, touched me upon the arm, and with a peculiar sound, signified that I must be silent and listen.

This I did do, but I heard nothing save the continued clattering of the rain, and after a while I said so.

For some time the Indian made no reply, although I was conscious that he was intensely interested in the prevailing dull sounds without.

Suddenly he sprang upon his feet and groped his way to the door. The intrusive noise awoke the woodchopper, who instantly seizing his rifle, sang out:

"Halloo, what's the matter, you red varmint, snorting in a man's face like a scared buffalo bull, what's the matter?"

"*River too near*," was the slow reply of the Indian.

"He's right, so help me ——," shouted the woodchopper, "the banks of the Mississippi ar caving in," and then with a spring he leaped through the door and bid us follow.

His advice was quickly obeyed. The Indian was the last to leave the cabin, and as he stepped from its threshold, the weighty unhewn logs that composed it, crumbled, along with the rich soil, into the swift-running current of the mysterious river.

This narrow escape made our fortunes somewhat bearable, and we waited with some little patience for day.

At the proper time the sun rose gloriously bright, as if its smiling face had never been obscured by a cloud.

The little birds of the woods sung merrily, there

was the freshness and beauty of a new creation on every thing; and the landscape of the previous night was indeed altered. The long jutting point where stood the squatter's hut and " clearing," had disappeared—house, garden-spot, fields, and fences, were obliterated; the water-washed banks were lined only with the unbroken forest.

The stranger, while looking, would never have dreamed that the axe and the plough had been in the vicinity.

The caving banks had swept away all signs of humanity, and left every thing about us in wild and primitive solitude.

GRIZZLY BEAR-HUNTING.

THE every-day sports of the wild woods include many feats of daring which never find a pen of record. Constantly, in the haunts of the savage, are being enacted scenes of thrilling interest, the very details of which, would make the denizen of enlightened life turn away with instinctive dread.

Every Indian tribe has its heroes; celebrated respectively for their courage, in different ways exhibited. Some, for their acuteness in pursuing the enemy on the war-path; and others, for the destruction they have accomplished among the wild beasts of the forest.

A great hunter, among the Indians, is a marked personage. It is a title that distinguishes its possessor among his people as a prince; while the trophies of exploits in which he has been engaged, hang about his person as brilliantly as the decorations of so many orders.

The country in which the Osage finds a home possesses abundantly the grizzly bear, an animal formidable beyond any other inhabitant of the North American forests—an animal seemingly insensible to pain, uncertain in its habits, and by its mighty strength able to overcome any living obstacle that comes within its reach, as an enemy.   The Indian warrior, of any tribe, among the haunts of the grizzly bear, finds no necklace so honorable to be worn as one formed of the claws of this gigantic animal, slain by his own prowess; and if he can add an eagle's plume to his scalp-lock, plucked from a bird shot while on the wing, he is honorable indeed.

The Indian's " smoke," like the fire-side of the white man, is often the place where groups of people assemble to relate whatever may most pleasantly while away the hours of a long evening, or break the monotony of a dull and idle day.   On such occasions, the old " brave " will sometimes relax from his natural gravity, and grow loquacious over his chequered life.   But no recital commands such undivided attention as the adventures with the grizzly bear—even the death of an enemy on the war-path hardly vies with it in interest.

We have listened to these soul-stirring adventures over the urn, or while lounging on the sofa; and the recital of the risks run—the hardships endured—have made us think them almost impossible, when compared with the conventional self-indulgence of enlightened life. But they were the tales of a truthful man—a hunter—

who had strayed away from the scenes once necessary for his life, and who loved, like the worn-out soldier, to "fight the battles over," in which he was once engaged.

It may be, and is the province of the sportsman to exaggerate—but the "hunter," surrounded by the magnificence and sublimity of an American forest, earning his bread by the hardy adventures of the chase, meets with too much reality to find room for coloring—too much of the sublime and terrible in the scenes with which he is associated to be boastful of himself. While apart from the favorable effects of civilization, he is also separated from its contaminations; *and boasting and exaggeration are settlement weaknesses*, and not the products of the wild woods.

The hunter, whether Indian or white, presents one of the most extraordinary exhibitions of the singular capacity of the human senses to be improved by cultivation. We are accustomed to look with surprise upon the instincts of animals and insects. We wonder and admire the sagacity they display, for the purposes of self-preservation—both in attack and defence. The lion, the bear, the beaver, the bee, all betray a species of intelligence, that seems for their particular purposes superior to the wisdom of man; yet, on examination, it will be found that this is not the case. For all histories of the human denizen of the forest show, that the Indian surpasses the brute in sagacity, while the white hunter excels both animal and savage.

The unfortunate deaf, dumb, and blind girl, in one of our public institutions,* selects her food, her clothing, and her friends, by the touch alone—so delicate has it become, from the mind's being directed to that sense alone.

The forest hunter is compelled by circumstances to cultivate his sight, to almost the same degree of perfection characterizing the blind girl's touch, and experience at last renders it so keen, that the slightest touch of a passing object on the leaves, trees, or earth, leaves to him a deep and visible impression, though to the common eye unseen as the path of the bird through the air. This knowledge governs the chase and the war-path; this knowledge is what, when excelled in, makes the master-spirit among the rude inhabitants of the woods: and that man is the greatest chief, who follows the coldest trail, and leaves none behind him by his own footsteps.

The hunter in pursuit of the grizzly bear is governed by this *instinct of sight*—it guides him with more certainty than the hound is directed by his nose. The impressions of the bear's footsteps upon the leaves, its marks on the trees, its resting-places, are all known long before the bear is really seen; and the hunter, while thus following "the trail," calculates the very sex, weight, and age with certainty. Thus it is that he will

* Hartford Asylum for the Deaf and Dumb.

neglect, or choose a trail—for in those indistinct paths, are visible to his mind's eye, bear that are young and old, lean and fat. You look into the forest, all is vacant; the hunter, at a casual glance, detects where has passed his object of pursuit, and grows as enthusiastic over this spiritual representation as if the reality was before him—and herein, perhaps, lies the distinction between the sportsman, and the huntsman. The hunter follows his object by his own knowledge and instinct, while the sportsman employs the instinct of domesticated animals to assist in his pursuits.

The different methods by which to destroy the grizzly bear, by those who hunt them, are as numerous as the bears that are killed. They are not animals which permit of a system in hunting them; and it is for this reason that they are so dangerous and difficult to destroy. The experience of one hunt may cost a limb or a life in the next one, if used as a criterion; and fatal, indeed, is a mistake,—when you grapple with an animal, whose gigantic strength enables him to lift a horse in his huge arms, and bear it away as a prize. There is one terrible exception to this rule; one habit of the animal may be certainly calculated upon, but a daring heart only can take advantage of it.

The grizzly bear, like the tiger and lion, have their caves in which they live; but they use them principally as a safe lodging-place when the cold of winter renders them torpid and disposed to sleep. To these caves they retire late in the fall, and they seldom venture out until awakened by the genial warmth of spring. Sometimes two occupy one cave, but this is not often the case, as the unsociability of the animal is proverbial, it preferring to be solitary and alone.

A knowledge of the forests, and an occasional trailing for bear, informs the hunter of these caves; and the only habit of the grizzly bear that can with certainty be taken advantage of, is the one of his being in his cave at the proper season. And the hunter has the terrible liberty of entering this den single-handed, and there destroying him. Of this only method of hunting the grizzly bear we would attempt a description.

The thought of entering a cave, inhabited by one of the most powerful beasts of prey, is calculated to try the strength of the stoutest nerves; and when it is considered that the least trepidation, the slightest mistake, may cause, and probably will result, in the instant death of the hunter, it certainly exhibits the highest demonstration of physical courage to pursue such a method of hunting. Yet there are many persons in the forests of North America who engage in such perilous adventures with no other object in view than the " *sport* " or a hearty meal.

The hunter's preparations to " beard the lion in his den," commence with examining the mouth of the cave he is about to enter. Upon the signs there exhibited, he decides whether the bear be alone; for if there be two, the cave is never entered. The size of the bear is also thus known, and the time since he was last in search of food.

The way that this knowledge is obtained, from indications so slight, or unseen to an ordinary eye, is one of the greatest mysteries of the woods.

Placing ourselves at the mouth of the cave containing a grizzly bear, to our untutored senses, there would be nothing to distinguish it from one that is unoccupied; but let some Diana of the forest touch our eyes, and give us the *instinct of sight* possessed by the hunter, and we would argue thus:

" From all the marks about the mouth of the cave, the occupant has not been out for a great length of time, for the grass and the earth have not been lately disturbed.

" The bear is in the cave, for the last tracks made are with the toe-marks towards it.

" There is but one bear, because the tracks are regular and of the same size.

" He is a large animal; the length of the step and the size of the paw indicate this.

"And he is fat, because his *hind feet do not step in the impressions made by the fore ones*, as is always the case with a lean bear."

Such are the signs and arguments that present themselves to the hunter; and mysterious as they seem, when not understood, when once explained, they strike

the imagination as being founded on the unerring simplicity and certainty of nature.

It may be asked, how is it that the grizzly bear is so
formidable to numbers when met in the forest, but when
in a cave can be assailed successfully by a single man?
In answer to this, we must recollect that the bear is
only attacked in his cave when he is in total darkness,
and suffering from surprise and the torpidity of the
season.

These three things are in this method of hunting
taken advantage of; and but for these advantages, no
quickness of eye, steadiness of nerve or forest experience, would protect for an instant, the intruder to the
cave of the grizzly bear.

The hunter, having satisfied himself about the cave,
prepares a candle, which he makes out of the wax taken
from the comb of wild bees, softened by the grease of
the bear. This candle has a large wick, and emits a
brilliant flame. Nothing else is needed but the rifle.
The knife and the belt are useless; for if a struggle
should ensue that would make it available, the foe is too
powerful to mind its thrusts before the hand using it
would be dead.

Bearing the candle before him, with the rifle in a
convenient position, the hunter fearlessly enters the
cave. He is soon surrounded by darkness, and is totally unconscious where his enemy will reveal himself.
Having fixed the candle in the ground in firm position,

with a provided apparatus, he lights it, and its brilliant flame soon penetrates into the recesses of the cavern— its size of course, rendering the illumination more or less complete.

The hunter now places himself on his belly, having the candle between the back part of the cave where the bear sleeps, and himself; in this position, with the muzzle of the rifle protruding out in front of him, he patiently waits for his victim. A short time only elapses before Bruin is aroused by the light. The noise made by his starting from sleep attracts the hunter, and he soon distinguishes the black mass; moving, stretching, and yawning like a person awaked from a deep sleep.

The hunter moves not, but prepares his rifle; the bear, finally aroused, turns his head towards the candle, and, with slow and waddling steps, approaches it.

Now is the time that tries the nerves of the hunter; it is too late to retreat, and his life hangs upon his certain aim and the goodness of his powder. The slightest variation in the bullet, or a flashing pan, and he is a doomed man.

So tenacious of life is the common black bear, that it is frequently wounded in its most vital parts, and still will escape, or give terrible battle.

But the grizzly bear seems to possess an infinitely greater tenacity of life. His skin, covered by matted hair, and the huge bones of his body, protect the heart as if incased in a wall; while the brain is buried in a skull, compared to which, adamant is not harder. A bullet, striking the bear's forehead, would flatten, if it struck squarely on the solid bone, as if fired against a rock; and dangerous indeed would it be to take the chance of reaching the animal's heart.

With these fearful odds against the hunter, the bear approaches the candle, growing every moment more sensible of some uncommon intrusion. He reaches the blaze, and raises his paw to strike it, or lifts his nose to scent it,—either of which will extinguish it, and leave the hunter and the bear in total darkness.

This dreadful moment is taken advantage of—the loud report of the rifle fills the cave with stunning noise —and as the light disappears, the ball, if successfully fired, penetrates the eye of the huge animal—the only place where it would find a passage to the brain; and this not only gives the death-wound, but instantly paralyzes, that no temporary resistance may be made.

On such fearful chances the American hunter perils his life, and often thoughtlessly, courts the danger.

A PIANO IN ARKANSAS.

WE shall never forget the excitement which seized upon the inhabitants of the little village of Hardscrabble, as the report spread through the community, that a real piano had actually arrived within its precincts.

Speculation was afloat as to its appearance and its use. The name was familiar to every body; but what it precisely meant, no one could tell. That it had legs was certain;—for a stray volume of some literary traveller was one of the most conspicuous works in the floating library of Hardscrabble; and said traveller stated, that he had seen a piano somewhere in New England with pantalettes on—also, an old foreign paper was brought forward, in which there was an advertisement headed " Soiree," which informed the " citizens generally," that Mr. Bobolink would preside at the piano.

This was presumed by several wiseacres, who had been to a menagerie, to mean, that Mr. Bobolink stirred the piano up with a long pole, in the same way that the showman did the lions and rhi-no-ce-rus.

7

So, public opinion was in favor of its being an animal, though a harmless one; for there had been a land speculator through the village a few weeks previously, who distributed circulars of a " Female Academy," for the accomplishment of young ladies. These circulars distinctly stated " the use of the piano to be one dollar per month."

One knowing old chap said, if they would tell him what so-i-ree meant, he would tell them what a piano was, and no mistake.

The owner of this strange instrument was no less than a very quiet and very respectable late merchant of a little town somewhere " north," who having failed at home, had emigrated into the new and hospitable country of Arkansas, for the purpose of bettering his fortune, and escaping the heartless sympathy of his more lucky neighbors, who seemed to consider him a very bad and degraded man because he had become honestly poor.

The new comers were strangers, of course. The house in which they were setting up their furniture was too little arranged " to admit of calls;" and as the family seemed very little disposed to court society, all prospects of immediately solving the mystery that hung about the piano seemed hopeless. In the mean time public opinion was " rife."

The depository of this strange thing was looked upon by the passers-by with indefinable awe; and as noises unfamiliar, sometimes reached the street, it was presumed that the piano made them, and the excitement rose higher than ever—in the midst of it, one or two old ladies, presuming upon their age and respectability, called upon the strangers and inquired after their health, and offered their services and friendship; meantime every thing in the house was eyed with the greatest intensity, but seeing nothing strange, a hint was given about the piano. One of the new family observed carelessly, " that it had been much injured by bringing out, that the damp had affected its tones, and that one of its legs was so injured that it would not stand up, and for the present it would not ornament the parlor."

Here was an explanation, indeed: injured in bringing out—damp affecting its tones—leg broken. " Poor thing!" ejaculated the old ladies with real sympathy, as they proceeded homeward; " travelling has evidently fatigued it; the Mass-is-sip fogs have given it a cold, poor thing!" and they wished to see it with increased curiosity.

The " village" agreed, that if Moses Mercer, familiarly called Mo Mercer," was in town, they would have a description of the piano, and the uses to which it was put; and fortunately, in the midst of the excitement, " Mo" arrived, he having been temporarily absent on a hunting expedition.

Moses Mercer was the only son of " old Mercer," who was, and had been, in the State Senate ever since

Arkansas was admitted into the " Union." Mo, from this fact, received great glory, of course; his father's greatness alone would have stamped him with supe-riority; but his having been twice to the " Capitol" when the legislature was in session, stamped his claims to pre-eminence over all competitors.

Mo Mercer was the oracle of the renowned village of Hardscrabble.

" Mo" knew every thing; he had all the consequence and complacency of a man who had never seen his equal, and never expected to. " Mo" bragged exten-sively upon his having been to the " Capitol" twice,— of his there having been in the most " fashionable soci-ety,"—of having seen the world. His return to town was therefore received with a shout. The arrival of the piano was announced to him, and *he alone* of all the community, was not astonished at the news

His insensibility was considered wonderful. He treated the piano as a thing that he was used to, and went on, among other things to say, that he had seen more pianos in the " Capitol " than he had ever seen woodchucks; and that it was not an animal, but a musi-cal instrument, played upon by the ladies; and he wound up his description by saying that the way " the dear creeters could pull music out of it was a caution to hoarse owls."

The new turn given to the piano excitement in Hardscrabble by Mo Mercer, was like pouring oil on

A PIANO IN ARKANSAS.   149

fire to extinguish it, for it blazed out with more vigor
than ever.   That it was a musical instrument, made it a
rarer thing in that wild country than if it had been an
animal, and people of all sizes, colors, and degrees, were
dying to see and hear it.

Jim Cash was Mo Mercer's right-hand man; in the
language of refined society, he was " Mo's toady,"—in
the language of Hardscrabble, he was " Mo's wheel-
horse."   Cash believed in Mo Mercer with an abandonment that was perfectly ridiculous.   Mr. Cash was dying to see the piano, and the first opportunity he had
alone with his Quixote, he expressed the desire that
was consuming his vitals.

" We'll go at once and see it," said Mercer.

" Strangers! " echoed the frightened Cash.

' Humbug! Do you think I have visited the 'Capitol' twice, and don't know how to treat fashionable society ?   Come along at once, Cash," said Mercer.

Off the pair started, Mercer all confidence, and Cash
all fears, as to the propriety of the visit.   These fears
Cash frankly expressed; but Mercer repeated, for the
thousandth time, his experience in the fashionable society of the " Capitol, and pianos," which he said " was
synonymous"—and he finally told Cash, to comfort him,
that however abashed and ashamed he might be in the
presence of the ladies, " that he needn't fear of sticking,
for he would pull him through."

A few minutes' walk brought the parties on the

broad galleries of the house that contained the object of so much curiosity. The doors and windows were closed, and a suspicious look was on every thing.

"Do they always keep a house closed up this way that has a piano in it?" asked Cash, mysteriously.

"Certainly," replied Mercer; "the damp would destroy its tones."

Repeated knocks at the doors, and finally at the windows, satisfied both Cash and Mercer that nobody was at home. In the midst of their disappointment, Cash discovered a singular machine at the end of the gallery, crossed by bars and rollers, and surmounted with an enormous crank. Cash approached it on tiptoe; he had a presentiment that he beheld the object of his curiosity, and as its intricate character unfolded itself, he gazed with distended eyes, and asked Mercer, with breathless anxiety, "What that strange and incomprehensible box was?"

Mercer turned to the thing as coolly as a north wind to an icicle, and said "that was *it*."

"That IT!!" exclaimed Cash, opening his eyes still wider; and then recovering himself, he asked to see "the tones."

Mercer pointed to the cross-bars and rollers. With trembling hands, with a resolution that would enable a man to be scalped without winking, Cash reached out his hand, and seized the handle of the crank (Cash, at heart, was a brave and fearless man); he gave it a turn, the machinery grated harshly, and seemed to clamor for something to be put in its maw.

"What delicious sounds!" said Cash.

"Beautiful!" observed the complacent Mercer, at the same time seizing Cash's arm, and asking him to desist, for fear of breaking the instrument, or getting it out of tune.

The simple caution was sufficient; and Cash, in the joy of the moment, at what he had done and seen, looked as conceited as Mo Mercer himself.

Busy, indeed, was Cash, from this time forward, in explaining to gaping crowds the exact appearance of the piano, how he had actually taken hold of it, and, as his friend Mo Mercer observed, "pulled music out of it."

The curiosity of the village was thus allayed, and consequently died comparatively away; Cash, however, having risen to almost as much importance as Mo Mercer, for having seen and handled the thing.

Our "Northern family" knew little or nothing of all this excitement; they received meanwhile the visits and congratulations of the hospitable villagers, and resolved to give a grand party to return some of the kindness they had received, and the piano was, for the first time, moved into the parlor. No invitation on this occasion was neglected; early at the post was every visitor, for it was rumored that Miss Patience Doolittle would, in the course of the evening, "perform on the piano."

The excitement was immense. The supper was passed over with a contempt, rivalling that which is cast
upon an excellent farce played preparatory to a dull
tragedy, in which the *star* is to appear. The furniture
was all critically examined; but nothing could be discovered answering Cash's description. An enormously
thick-leafed table, with a "spread" upon it, attracted
little attention, *timber* being so very cheap in a new
country, and so every body expected soon to see the
piano "brought in."

Mercer, of course, was the hero of the evening;
he talked much and loudly. Cash, as well as several
young ladies, went into hysterics at his wit. Mercer,
as the evening wore away, grew exceedingly conceited,
even for him; and he graciously asserted that the company present reminded him of his two visits to the "Capitol," and other associations, equally exclusive and peculiar.

The evening wore on apace, and still—no piano. That
hope deferred which maketh the heart sick, was felt by
some elderly ladies, and by a few younger ones; and
Mercer was solicited to ask Miss Patience Doolittle, to
favor the company with the presence of the piano.

"Certainly," said Mercer, and with the grace of a
city dandy he called upon the lady to gratify all present
with a little music, prefacing his request with the remark,
that if she was fatigued, "his friend Cash would give the
machine a *turn*."

Darley Del.   Gilbert. Sc.

" She approached the *thick leafed table*, and removed the covering, throwing
it carelessly and gracefully aside."—*page* 153.

Miss Patience smiled, and looked at Cash.

Cash's knees trembled.

All eyes in the room turned upon him.

Cash sweat all over.

Miss Patience said she was gratified to hear that Mr. Cash was a musician ; she admired people who had a musical taste. Whereupon Cash fell into a chair, as he afterwards observed, " chawed-up."

Oh that Beau Brummel, or any of his admirers could have seen Mo Mercer all this while ! Calm as a summer morning—complacent as a newly-painted sign—he smiled and patronized, and was the only unexcited person in the room.

Miss Patience rose,—a sigh escaped from all present,—the piano was evidently to be brought in. She approached the thick-leafed table, and removed the covering, throwing it carelessly and gracefully aside ; opened the instrument, and presented the beautiful arrangement of dark and white keys.

Mo Mercer at this, for the first time in his life, looked confused ; he was Cash's authority in his descriptions of the appearance of the piano ; while Cash himself, began to recover the moment that he ceased to be an object of attention. Many a whisper now ran through the room as to the "tones," and more particularly the " crank ;" none could see them.

Miss Patience took her seat, ran her fingers over a few octaves, and if "Moses in Egypt" was not perfectly

7*

executed, Moses in Hardscrabble *was*. The dulcet sounds ceased. "Miss," said Cash, the moment that he could express himself, so entranced was he by the music,—"Miss Doolittle, what was that instrument Mo Mercer showed me in your gallery once, that went by a crank, and had rollers in it?"

It was now the time for Miss Patience to blush; so away went the blood from confusion to her cheeks; she hesitated, stammered, and said, "if Mr. Cash must know, it was a—a—a—*Yankee washing machine.*"

The name grated on Mo Mercer's ears as if rusty nails had been thrust into them; the heretofore invulnerable Mercer's knees trembled; the sweat started to his brow as he heard the taunting whispers of "visiting the Capitol twice," and seeing pianos as plenty as wood-chucks.

The fashionable vices of envy and maliciousness, were that moment sown in the village of Hardscrabble; and Mo Mercer—the great—the confident—the happy and self-possessed—surprising as it may seem, was the first victim sacrificed to their influence.

Time wore on, and pianos became common, and Mo Mercer less popular; and he finally disappeared altogether, on the evening of the day on which a Yankee peddler of notions sold, to the highest bidder, "six patent, warranted, and improved Mo Mercer pianos."

WILD-CAT HUNTING.

In the southern portions of the United States, but especially in Louisiana, the wild-cat is found in abundance. The dense swamps that border on the Mississippi, protect this vicious species of game from extermination, and foster their increase ; and, although every year vast numbers are killed, they remain seemingly as numerous as they ever were " in the memory of the oldest inhabitant."

The wild-cat seeks the most solitary retreats in which to rear its young, where in some natural hole in the ground, or some hollow tree, it finds protection for itself and its kittens from the destructive hand of man. At night, or early morn, it comes abroad, stealing over the dried leaves, in search of prey, as quietly as a zephyr, or ascending the forest tree with almost the ease of a bird.

The nest on the tree, and the burrow in the ground are alike invaded; while the poultry-yard of the farmer, and his sheepfold, are drawn on liberally, to supply the cat with food.   It hunts down the rabbit, coon, and possum, and springs from the elevated bough upon the bird perched beneath, catching in its mouth its victim; and will do this while descending like an arrow in speed, and with the softness of a feather to the ground. Nothing can exceed its beauty of motion when in pursuit of game, or sporting in play.   No leap seems too formidable—no attitude ungraceful.   It runs—flies— leaps—skips—and is at ease, in an instant of time; every hair of its body seems redolent with life.

Its disposition is untamable; it seems insensible to kindness; a mere mass of ill-nature, having no sympathies with any, not even of its own kind.   It is for this reason, no doubt, that it is so recklessly pursued; its paw being, like the hand of the Ishmaelite, against every man; and it most indubitably follows, that every man's dogs, sticks, and guns, are against it.   The hounds themselves, that hunt equally well the cat and the fox, pursue the former with a clamorous joy, and kill it with a zest which they do not display when finishing off a fine run after Reynard.   In fact, as an animal of sport, the cat in many respects is preferable to the fox; its trail is always warmer, and it shows more sagacity in eluding its enemies.

In Louisiana the sportsman starts out in the morning, professedly for a fox-chase, and it turns out " cat," and often both cat and fox are killed, after a short but hard morning's work.

The chase is varied, and is frequently full of amusing incident, for the cat, as might be expected, will take to the trees, to avoid pursuit, and this habit of the animal allows the sportsman to meet it on quite familiar terms. If the tree be a tall one, the excitable creature manages to have its face obscured by the distance ; but if it takes to a dead, limbless trunk, where the height will permit its head to be fairly seen, as it looks down upon the pack that, with such open mouths,

" Fetch shrill echoes from the hollow earth,"

you will see a rare exhibition of rage and fury ; eyes that seem like living balls of fire, poisonous claws, which clutch the insensible wood with deep indentations ; the foam trembles on its jaws ; the hair stands up like porcupine quills ; the cars press down to the head, forming as perfect a picture of vicious, ungovernable destructiveness as can be imagined. A charge of mustard-seed shot, or a poke with a stick when at bay, will cause it to desert its airy abode ; and it no sooner touches the ground, than it breaks off at a killing pace, the pack like mad fiends on its trail.

Besides " treeing," the cat will take advantage of some hole in the ground, and disappear, when it meets with these hiding-places, as suddenly as ghosts vanish at cock-crowing. The hounds come up to the hiding-place, and a fight ensues. The first head intruded into the cat's hole is sure to meet with a warm reception. Claws and teeth do their work.

Still the staunch hound heeds it not, and either he gets a hold himself, or acts as a bait to draw the cat from its burrow ; thus fastened, the dog, being the most powerful in strength, backs out, dragging his enemy along with him ; and no sooner is the cat's head seen by the rest of the pack, than they pounce upon it, and in a few moments the " nine lives " of the " varmint " are literally *chawed-up*.

At one of these burrowings, a huge cat intruded into a hole so small, that an ordinarily large hound could not follow. A little stunted but excellent dog, rejoicing in the name of Ringwood, from his diminutiveness succeeded in forcing his way into the hole after the cat ; in an instant a faint scream was heard, and the little fellow gave symptoms of having caught a Tartar. One of the party present stooped down, and running his arm under the dog's body, pressed it forward, until he could feel that the cat had the dog firmly clawed by each shoulder, with his nose in the cat's mouth ; in this situation, by pressing the dog firmly under the chest, the two were drawn from the hole.

The cat hung on until he discovered that his victim was surrounded by numerous friends, when he let go his cruel hold, the more vigorously to defend himself. Ringwood, though covered with jetting blood, jumped upon the cat, and shook away as if unharmed in the contest.

Sportsmen, in hunting the cat, provide themselves generally with pistols—not for the purpose of killing the cat, but to annoy it, so that it will leap from the tree, when it has taken to one. Sometimes from negligence these infantile shooting-irons are left at home, and the cat gets safely out of the reach of sticks, or whatever other missile may be convenient. This is a most provoking affair; dogs and sportsmen lose all patience; and as no expedient suggests itself, the cat escapes for the time.

I once knew a cat thus perched out of reach, that was brought to terms in a very singular manner.

The tree on which the animal was lodged being a very high one, and secure from all interruption, it looked down upon its pursuers with the most provoking complacency; every effort to dislodge it had failed, and the hunt was about to be abandoned in despair, when one of the sportsmen discovered a grape-vine that passed directly over the cat's body, and by running his eyes along its circumvolutions, traced it down to the ground; a judicious jerk at the vine touched the cat on the rump; this was most unexpected, and it instantly leaped to the ground from a height of over forty feet; striking on its fore paws, and throwing a sort of rough somerset, it started off as sound in limb and wind, as if he had just jumped from a " hucklebury " bush.

The hunter of the wild turkey, while "calling," in imitation of the hen, to allure the gobbler within reach of his gun, will sometimes be annoyed by the appearance of the wild-cat stealing up to the place from whence the sounds proceed.   The greatest caution on such occasions is visible in the cat; it progresses by the slowest possible movements, crawling along like a serpent.   The hunter knows that the intruder has spoiled his turkey sport for the morning, and his only revenge is to wait patiently, and give the cat the contents of his gun, then, minus all game, he goes home anathematizing the whole race of cats, for thus interfering with his sport and his dinner.

Of all the peculiarities of the cat, its untameable and quarrelsome disposition, is its most marked character- istic.

There is no half-way mark, no exception, no occa- sional moment of good nature; starvation and a surfeit, blows and kind words, kicks, cuffs, and fresh meat, reach not the sympathies of the wild-cat.

He has all the greediness of a pawnbroker, the ill na- ture of a usurer, the meanness of a pettifogging lawyer, the blind rage of the hog, and the apparent insensibility to pain of the turtle : like a woman, the wild-cat is in- comparable with any thing but itself.

In expression of face, the wild-cat singularly resem- bles the rattlesnake.   The skulls of these two " varmints" have the same venomous expression, the same demonstration of fangs; and probably no two living creatures attack each other with more deadly ferocity and hate. They will stare at each other with eyes filled with defiance, and burning with fire; one hissing, and the other snarling; presenting a most terrible picture of the malevolence of passion.

The serpent in his attitudes is all grace—the cat, all activity. The serpent moves with the quickness of lightning while making the attack; the cat defends with motions equally quick, bounding from side to side, striking with its paws. Both are often victims, for they seldom separate until death-blows have been inflicted on either side.

The western hunter, when he wishes to cap the climax of braggadocio, with respect to his own prowess, says, "He can whip his weight in wild-cats." This is saying all that can be said, for it would seem, considering its size, that the cat in a fight can bite fiercer, scratch harder, and live longer than any other animal whatever.

"I am a roaring earthquake in a fight," sung out one of the half-horse, half-alligator species of fellows—"a real snorter of the universe. I can strike as hard as fourth proof lightning, and keep it up, rough and tumble, as long as a wild-cat."

These high encomiums on the character of the pugnacity of the cat are beyond question.

A "singed cat" is an excellent proverb, illustrating

that a person may be smarter than he looks.   A singed *wild*-cat, as such an illustration, would be sublime.

The Indians, who, in their notions and traditions, are always picturesque and beautiful, imagine that the rattlesnake, to live, must breathe the poisonous air of the swamps, and the exhalations of decayed animal matter ; while the cat has the attribute of gloating over the meaner displays of evil passions of a quarrelsome person ; for, speaking of a quarrelsome family, they say, " That the lodge containing it *fattens the wild-cat.*"

Mike Fink's Great Shot.

MIKE FINK, THE KEEL-BOATMAN.

OCCASIONALLY, may be seen on the Ohio and Mississippi rivers singularly hearty-looking men, who would puzzle a stranger, as to their history and age. Their bodies always exhibit a powerful development of muscle and bone; their cheeks are prominent, and you would pronounce them men enjoying perfect health in middle life, were it not for their heads, which, if not entirely bald, will be but sparsely covered with steel-gray hair.

Another peculiarity about this people is, that they have a singular knowledge of all the places on the river; every bar and bend is spoken of with precision and familiarity; every town is recollected before it was half as large as the present, or, "when it was no town at all." Innumerable places are marked out by them, where once was an Indian fight, or a rendezvous of robbers.

The manner, the language, and the dress of these

individuals are all characteristic of sterling common sense—the manner modest, yet full of self-reliance—the language strong and forcible, from superiority of mind, rather than from education—the dress studied for·comfort, rather than fashion—on the whole, you become attached to them and court their society. The good humor—the frankness—the practical sense—the reminiscences—the powerful frame—all indicate a character, at the present day anomalous; and such, indeed, is the case, for your acquaintance will be one of the few remaining people, now spoken of as the " Last of the keel-boatmen."

Thirty years ago the navigation of the Western waters was confined to this class of men; the obstacles presented to the pursuit of commerce in those swift-running and wayward waters had to be overcome by physical force alone; the navigator's arm grew strong as he guided his rude craft past the " snag " and " sawyer," or kept it off the no less dreaded " bar."

Besides all this, the deep forests that covered the river banks concealed the wily Indian, who gloated over the shedding of blood. The qualities of the frontier warrior, therefore, associated themselves with those of the boatman, while these men would, when at home, drop both these characters in that of cultivator of the soil.

It is no wonder, then, that they were brave, hardy, and open-handed men: their whole lives were a

round of manly excitement; they were, when most natural, hyperbolical in thought and in deed, if compared
with any other class of men. Their bravery and chivalrous deeds were performed without a herald to pro-
claim them to the world—they were the mere incidents
of a border life, considered too common to attract attention, or outlive the time of a passing wonder. Death
has nearly destroyed the men, and obscurity is fast ob-
literating the record of their deeds; but a few examples
still exist, as if to justify the truth of these wonderful
exploits, now almost wholly confined to tradition.

Among the flat-boatmen there were none who gained
more notoriety than *Mike Fink*. His name is still remembered along the whole of the Ohio, as a man who
excelled his fellows in every thing,—particularly in his
rifle-shot, which was acknowledged to be unsurpassed.
Probably no man ever lived, who could compete with
Mike in the latter accomplishment. Strong as Hercu-
les, free from all nervous excitement, possessed of perfect health, and familiar with his weapon from child-
hood; he raised the rifle to his eye, and, having once
taken sight, it was as firmly fixed as if buried in a
rock.

The rifle was Mike's pride, and he rejoiced on all occasions where he could bring it into use, whether it was
turned against the beast of prey or the more savage Indian: and in his day, the last named was the common
foe with whom Mike and his associates had to contend.

On the occasion when we would particularly intro-
duce Mike to the reader, he had bound himself for a
while to the pursuits of trade, until a voyage from the
head-waters of the Ohio, and down the Mississippi,
could be completed.   Heretofore he had kept himself
exclusively to the Ohio, but a liberal reward, and some
curiosity, prompted him to extend his business character beyond his ordinary habits and inclinations.

In the accomplishment of this object, he lolled
carelessly over the big " sweep" that guided the " flat "
on which he officiated ;—the current of the river bore the
boat swiftly along, and made his labor light.   Wild and
uncultivated as Mike appeared, he loved nature, and had
a soul that sometimes felt, while admiring it, an exalted
enthusiasm.

The beautiful Ohio was his favorite stream.   From
where it runs no stronger than a gentle rivulet, to where
it mixes with the muddy Mississippi, Mike was as
familiar with its meanderings, as a child could be with
those of a flower-garden.   He could not help noticing
with sorrow the desecrating hand of improvement as he
passed along, and half soliloquizing, and half addressing
his companions, he broke forth :

" I knew these parts afore a squatter's axe had
blazed a tree ; 'twasn't then pulling a —— sweep to
get a living ; but pulling the trigger, did the business.
Those were times to see ;—a man might call himself
lucky then.

" What's the use of improvements?

" When did cutting down trees make deer more plenty?

" Who ever found wild buffalo, or a brave Indian, in a city? Where's the fun, the frolicking, the fighting? Gone! Gone!

" The rifle won't make a man a living now—he must turn mule and work. If forests continue this way to be used up, I may yet be smothered in a settlement. Boys, this 'ere life won't do. I'll stick to the broad-horn 'cordin' to contract; but once done with it, I'm off for a frolic. If the Choctas or Cherokees on the Mississip don't give us a brush as we pass along, I shall grow as poor as a starved wolf in a pitfall.

" I must, to live peaceably, point my rifle at something more dangerous than varmint. Six months and no fight, would spile me worse than a 'tack of rheumatism."

Mike ceased speaking. The then beautiful village of Louisville appeared in sight; the labor of landing the boat occupied his attention—the bustle and confusion that followed such an incident ensued; and Mike was his own master by law, until his employers ceased trafficking, and again required his services.

At the time we write of, a great many renegade Indians lived about the settlements, which is still the case in the extreme southwest. These Indians are generally the most degraded of their tribe—outcasts, who, for crime or dissipation, are no longer allowed to associate with their people; they live by hunting or stealing, and spend, in the towns, their precarious gains in intoxication.

Among the throng that crowded on the flat-boat on his arrival, were a number of these unfortunate beings; they were influenced by no other motive than that of loitering round in idle speculation at what was going on.

Mike was attracted towards them at sight; and as he was idle, and consequently in the situation that is deemed most favorable to mischief, it struck him that it was a good opportunity to have a little sport at the Indians' expense.

Without ceremony, he gave a terrific war-whoop; and then mixing the language of the aborigines and his own together, he went on savage fashion, and bragged of his triumphs and victories on the war-path, with all the seeming earnestness of a real " brave." Nor were taunting words spared to exasperate the poor creatures, who, while perfectly helpless, listened to the tales of their own greatness, and their own shame, until wound up to the highest pitch of impotent exasperation. Mike's companions joined in; thoughtless boys caught the spirit of the affair; and the Indians were goaded until they, in turn, made battle with their tongues.

Then commenced a system of running against them, pulling off their blankets, joined with a thousand other

indignities; finally the Indians made a precipitate retreat ashore, amid the hooting and jeering of a thoughtless crowd which considered them as poor devils, destitute of both feeling and humanity.

Among this band of outcasts was a Cherokee, who
bore the name of Proud Joe; what his real cognomen
was, no one knew, for he was taciturn, haughty—and, in
spite of his poverty and his manner of life, won the name
we have mentioned. His face was expressive of talent,
but it was furrowed by the most terrible habits of
drunkenness. That he was a superior Indian was admitted: and it was also understood that he was banish-
ed from his mountain home, his tribe being then numerous and powerful, for some great crime. He was always
looked up to by his companions, and managed, however
intoxicated he might be, to sustain a singularly proud
bearing, which did not even depart from him while prostrate on the ground.

Joe was careless of his person and habits—in this
respect he was behind his fellows; but one ornament of
his, was attended to with a care which would have done
honor to him if still surrounded by his people, and amid
his native woods. Joe still wore, with Indian dignity,
his scalplock; he ornamented it with taste, and cherished
it, as report said, until some Indian messenger of ven-
geance should tear it from his head, as expiatory of his
numerous crimes. Mike had noticed this peculiarity;
and, reaching out his hand, plucked from the revered
scalplock a hawk's feather.   8

The Indian glared horribly on Mike as he consummated the insult, snatched the feather from his hand, then shaking his clenched fist in the air, as if calling on Heaven for revenge, retreated with his friends.

Mike saw that he had roused the soul of the savage, and he marvelled wonderfully that so much resentment should be exhibited; and as an earnest to Proud Joe that the wrong he had done him should not rest unrevenged, he swore that he would cut the scalplock off close to his head, the first convenient opportunity, and then he thought no more about it.

The morning following the arrival of the boat at Louisville was occupied in making preparations to pursue the voyage down the river. Nearly every thing was completed, and Mike had taken his favorite place at the sweep, when, looking up the river bank, he beheld at some distance Joe and his companions, and perceived, from their gesticulations, that they were making him the subject of conversation.

Mike thought instantly of several ways in which he could show them altogether, a fair fight, and then whip them with ease; he also reflected with what extreme satisfaction he would enter into the spirit of the arrangement, and other matters to him equally pleasing—when all the Indians disappeared, save Joe himself, who stood at times viewing Mike in moody silence, and then staring round at passing objects.

From the peculiarity of Joe's position to Mike, who

was below him, his head and the upper part of his body were relieved boldly against the sky, and in one of his movements, he brought his profile face to view. The prominent scalp-lock and its adornments seemed to be more striking than ever, and again roused the pugnacity of Mike Fink; in an instant he raised his rifle, always loaded and at command, brought it to his eye, and, before he could be prevented, drew sight upon Proud Joe, and fired. The ball whistled loud and shrill, and Joe, springing his whole length into the air, fell upon the ground.

The cold-blooded murder was noticed by fifty persons at least, and there arose from the crowd a universal cry of horror and indignation at the bloody deed. Mike, himself, seemed to be much astonished, and in an instant reloaded his rifle, and as a number of white persons rushed towards the boat, Mike threw aside his coat, and, taking his powder-horn between his teeth, leaped, rifle in hand, into the Ohio, and commenced swimming for the opposite shore.

Some bold spirits determined that Mike should not so easily escape, and jumping into the only skiff at command, pulled swiftly after him. Mike watched their movements until they came within a hundred yards of him, then turning in the water, he supported himself by his feet alone, and raised his deadly rifle to his eye. Its muzzle, if it spoke hostilely, was as certain to send a messenger of death through one or more of his pursuers, as if it were lightning, and they knew it; they dropped their oars, and silently returned to the shore. Mike waved his hand towards the little village of Louisville, and again pursued his way.

The time consumed by the firing of Mike's rifle, the pursuit, and the abandonment of it, required less time than we have taken to give the details; and in that time, to the astonishment of the gaping crowd around Joe, they saw him rising with a bewildered air; a moment more—he recovered his senses and stood up—*at his feet lay his scalp-lock!*

The ball had cut it clear from his head; the cord around the root, in which were placed feathers and other ornaments, still held it together; the concussion had merely stunned its owner; farther—he had escaped all bodily harm! A cry of exultation rose at the last evidence of the skill of Mike Fink—the exhibition of a shot that established his claim, indisputably, to the eminence he ever afterwards held—that of the unrivalled marksman of all the flatboatmen of the western waters.

Proud Joe had received many insults. He looked upon himself as a degraded, worthless being—and the ignominy heaped upon him he never, except by reply, resented; but this last insult was like seizing the lion by the mane, or a Roman senator by the beard—it roused the slumbering demon within, and made him again thirst to resent his wrongs, with an intensity of emotion that can only be felt by an Indian. His eye glared upon the jeering crowd like a fiend; his chest swelled and heaved until it seemed that he must suffocate.

No one noticed this emotion. All were intent upon the exploit that had so singularly deprived Joe of his war-lock; and, smothering his wrath, he retreated to his associates with a consuming fire at his vitals. He was a different being from what he had been an hour before; and with that desperate resolution on which a man stakes his all, he swore, by the Great Spirit of his forefathers, that he would be revenged.

An hour after the disappearance of Joe, both he and Mike Fink were forgotten. The flatboat, which the latter had deserted, was got under way, and dashing through the rapids in the river opposite Louisville, wended on its course. As is customary when night sets in, the boat was securely fastened in some little bend or bay in the shore, where it remained until early morn.

Long before the sun had fairly risen, the boat was again pushed into the stream, and it passed through a valley presenting the greatest possible beauty and freshness of landscape that the mind can conceive.

It was spring, and a thousand tints of green developed themselves in the half-formed foliage and bursting buds. The beautiful mallard skimmed across the water, ignorant of the danger of the white man's approach; the splendid spoon-bill decked the shallow places near the shore, while myriads of singing birds filled the air with their unwritten songs.

In the far reaches down the river, there occasionally might be seen a bear stepping along the ground as if dainty of its feet; and, snuffing the intruder on his wild home, he would retreat into the woods.

To enliven all this, and give the picture the look of humanity, there was also seen, struggling with the floating mists, a column of blue smoke, which came from a fire built on a projecting point of land, around which the current swept rapidly, hurrying past every thing that floated on the river. The eye of the boatmen saw the advantage which the situation of the place rendered to those on shore, to annoy and attack; and as wandering Indians, even in those days, did not hesitate to rob, there was much speculation as to what reception the boat would receive from the builders of the fire.

The rifles were all loaded, to be prepared for any kind of reception, and the loss of Mike Fink was lamented, as the prospect of a fight presented itself, where he could use with effect his terrible rifle. The boat in the mean time swept round the point; but instead of an enemy, there lay, in a profound sleep, Mike Fink, with his feet toasting at the fire, his pillow was a huge bear that had been shot on the day previous, while, scattered in profusion around him, were several deer and wild turkeys.

Mike had not been idle. After selecting a place most eligible for noticing the passing boat, he had spent his time in hunting,—and was surrounded by trophies of his prowess. The scene that he presented was worthy of the time and the man, and would have thrown Landseer into a delirium of joy, could he have witnessed it. The boat, owing to the swiftness of the current, passed Mike's resting-place, although it was pulled strongly to the shore. As Mike's companions came opposite to him, they raised a shout, half exultation at meeting him, and half to alarm him with the idea that Joe's friends were upon him. Mike, at the sound, sprang to his feet, rifle in hand, and as he looked around, he raised it to his eyes, and by the time that he discovered the boat, he was ready to fire.

"Down with your shooting-iron, you wild critter," shouted one of the boatmen.

Mike dropped the piece, and gave a loud halloo, which echoed among the solitudes like a piece of artillery. The meeting between Mike and his fellows was characteristic. They joked, and jibed him with their rough wit, and he parried it off with a most creditable ingenuity. Mike soon learned the extent of his rifle-shot—but he seemed perfectly indifferent to the fact that Proud Joe was not dead.

The only sentiment he uttered, was regret that he did not fire at the vagabond's head, for if he hadn't hit it, why, he said that he would have made the first bad shot in twenty years. The dead game was carried on board of the boat, the adventure was forgotten, and every thing resumed the monotony of floating in a flat-boat down the Ohio.

A month or more elapsed, and Mike had progressed several hundred miles down the Mississippi; his journey had been remarkably free from incident; morning, noon, and night, presented the same banks, the same muddy water, and he sighed to see some broken land, some high hills, and he railed and swore, that he should have been such a fool as to desert his favorite Ohio for a river that produced nothing but alligators; and was never, at best, half finished.

Occasionally, the plentifulness of game put him in spirits, but it did not last long; he wanted more lasting excitement, and declared himself as perfectly miserable and helpless, as a wild-cat without teeth or claws.

In the vicinity of Natchez rise a few abrupt hills, which tower above the surrounding lowlands of the Mississippi like monuments; they are not high, but from their loneliness and rarity, they create sensations of pleasure and awe.

Under the shadow of one of these bluffs, Mike and his associates made the customary preparations for passing the night. Mike's enthusiasm knew no bounds at the sight of land again; he said it was as pleasant as " cold water to a fresh wound;" and, as his spirits rose, he went on making the region round about, according to his notions, an agreeable residence.

" The Choctaws live in these diggins," said Mike, " and a cursed time they must have of it. Now if I lived in these parts I'd declare war on 'em just to have something to keep me from growing dull; without some such business I'd be as musty as an old swamp moccason snake. I would build a cabin on that ar hill yonder, and could, from its location, with my rifle, repulse a whole tribe, if they dar'd to come after me.

"What a beautiful time I'd have of it! I never was particular about what's called a fair fight; I just ask half a chance, and the odds against me,—and if I then don't keep clear of snags and. sawyers, let me spring a leak and go to the bottom. It's natur that the big fish should eat the little ones. I've seen trout swallow a perch, and a cat would come along and swallow the trout, and perhaps, on the Mississippi, the alligators use up the cat, and so on to the end of the row.

"Well, I will walk tall into varmint and Indian; it's a way I've got, and it comes as natural as grinning to a hyena. I'm a regular tornado—tough as a hickory— and long-winded as a nor'-wester. I can strike a blow like a falling tree—and every lick makes a gap in the crowd that lets in an acre of sunshine. Whew, boys!" shouted Mike, twirling his rifle like a walking-stick around his head, at the ideas suggested in his mind. "Whew, boys! if the Choctaw divils in them ar woods thar would give us a brush, just as I feel now, I'd call them gentlemen. I must fight something, or I'll catch the dry rot—burnt brandy won't save me."

Such were some of the expressions which Mike gave utterance to, and in which his companions heartily

8*

joined; but they never presumed to be quite equal to Mike,—for his bodily prowess, as well as his rifle, were acknowledged to be unsurpassed. These displays of animal spirits generally ended in boxing and wrestling-matches, in which falls were received, and blows struck without being noticed, that would have destroyed common men.

Occasionally, angry words and blows were exchanged, but, like the summer storm, the cloud that emitted the lightning also purified the air; and when the commotion ceased, the combatants immediately made friends, and became more attached to each other than before the cause that interrupted the good feelings occurred. Such were the conversation and amusements of the evening when the boat was moored under the bluffs we have alluded to.

As night wore on, one by one, the hardy boatmen fell asleep, some in its confined interior, and others, protected by a light covering in the open air.

The moon arose in beautiful majesty; her silver light, behind the highlands, gave them a power and theatrical effect as it ascended; and as its silver rays grew perpendicular, they kissed gently the summit of the hills, and poured down their full light upon the boat, with almost noonday brilliancy. The silence with which the beautiful changes of darkness and light were produced, made it mysterious. It seemed as if some creative power was at work, bringing form and life out of darkness.

But in the midst of the witchery of this quiet scene, there sounded forth the terrible rifle, and the more terrible war-whoop of the Indian. One of the boatmen, asleep on deck, gave a stifled groan, turned upon his face, and with a quivering motion, ceased to live.

Not so with his companions—they in an instant, as men accustomed to danger and sudden attacks, sprang ready-armed to their feet ; but before they could discover their foes, seven sleek and horribly painted savages, leaped from the hill into the boat. The firing of the rifle was useless, and each man singled out a foe, and met him with the drawn knife.

The struggle was quick and fearful ; and deadly blows were given, amid screams and imprecations that rent the air. Yet the voice of Mike Fink could be heard in encouraging shouts above the clamor.

"Give it to them, boys !" he cried, " cut their hearts out ! choke the dogs ! Here's h—ll a-fire and the river rising !" Then clenching with the most powerful of the assailants, he rolled with him upon the deck of the boat. Powerful as Mike was, the Indian seemed nearly a match for him. The two twisted and writhed like serpents,—now one seeming to have the advantage, and then the other.

In all this confusion there might occasionally be seen glancing in the moonlight the blade of a knife ; but at whom the thrusts were made, or who wielded it, could not be discovered.

The general fight lasted less time than we have taken to describe it. The white men gained the advantage; two of the Indians lay dead upon the boat, and the living, escaping from their antagonists, leaped ashore, and before the rifle could be brought to bear, they were out of its reach.

While Mike was yet struggling with his adversary, one of his companions cut the boat loose from the shore, and, with powerful exertion, managed to get its bows so far into the current, that it swung round and floated; but before this was accomplished, and before any one interfered with Mike, he was on his feet, covered with blood, and blowing like a porpoise : by the time that he could get his breath, he commenced talking.

"Ain't been so busy in a long time," said he, turning over his victim with his foot; "that fellow fou't beautiful; if he's a specimen of the Choctaws that live in these parts, they are screamers; the infernal sarpents ! the d——d possums !"

Talking in this way, he with others, took a general survey of the killed and wounded. Mike himself was a good deal cut up with the Indian's knife; but he called his wounds—blackberry scratches. One of Mike's associates was severely hurt; the rest escaped comparatively harmless. The sacrifice was made at the first fire; for beside the dead Indians, there lay one of the boat's crew, cold and dead, his body perforated with four different balls. That he was the chief object of attack seemed evident, yet no one of his associates knew of his ever having had a single fight with the Indians.

The soul of Mike was affected, and, taking the hand of his deceased comrade between his own, he raised his bloody knife towards the bright moon, and swore that he would desolate "the nation" of the Indians who made war upon them that night; and turning to his stiffened victim, which still retained the expression of implacable hatred and defiance, he gave it a smile of grim satisfaction, and then joined in the general conversation which the occurrences of the night would naturally suggest.

The master of the "broad horn" was a business man, and had often been down the Mississippi. This was the first attack he had received, or knew to have been made from the shores inhabited by the Choctaws, except by the white man; and he suggested the keeping the dead Indians until daylight, that they might have an opportunity to examine their dress and features, and see with certainty, who were to blame for the occurrences of the night.

The dead boatman was removed with care to a respectful distance; and the living, except the person at the sweep of the boat, were soon buried in profound slumber.

Not until after the rude breakfast was partaken of, and the funeral rites of the dead boatman were solemnly performed, did Mike and his companions disturb the corses of the red men.

Mike went about his business with alacrity. He stripped the bloody blanket from the Indian he had killed, as if it enveloped something requiring no respect. He examined carefully the moccasons on the Indian's feet, pronouncing them at one time Chickasas—at another time, Shawnese. He stared at the livid face, but could not recognize the style of paint.

That the Indians were not strictly national in their adornments, was certain, for they were examined by practised eyes, that could have told the nation of the dead, if such had been the case, as readily as a sailor distinguishes a ship by its flag. Mike was evidently puzzled; and as he was about giving up his task as hopeless, the dead body he was examining was turned upon its side. Mike's eyes distended, as some of his companions observed, " like a choked cat's," and became riveted.

He drew himself up in a half serious, and half comic expression, and pointing at the back of the dead Indian's head, there was exhibited a dead warrior in his paint, destitute of his scalp-lock—the small stump which was only left, being stiffened with *red paint*. Those who could read Indian symbols learned a volume of deadly resolve in what they saw. The body of Proud Joe, was stiff and cold before them.

The last and best shot of Mike Fink had cost a brave man his life. The boatman so lately interred was evidently taken in the moonlight by Proud Joe and his party for Mike Fink, and they had risked their lives, one and all, that he might with certainty be sacrificed.

Nearly a thousand miles of swamp had been threaded, large and swift running rivers had been crossed, hostile tribes passed through by Joe and his friends, that they might revenge the fearful insult of destroying, *without the life*, the sacred scalp-lock.

ALLIGATOR KILLING.

In the dark recesses of the loneliest swamps—in those dismal abodes where production and decay run riot—where the serpent crawls from his den among the tangled ferns and luxuriant grass, and hisses forth, unmolested, his propensities to destroy—where the toad and lizard spend the livelong day in their melancholy chirpings—where the stagnant pool festers and ferments, and bubbles up its foul miasma—where the fungi seem to grow beneath your gaze—where the unclean birds retire after their repast, and sit and stare with dull eyes in vacancy for hours and days together;—there originates the alligator; there, if happy in his history, he lives and dies.

But, alas! the pioneer of the forest invades his home —the axe lets in the sunshine upon his hiding-places :— and he frequently finds himself, like the Indian, surrounded by the encroachments of civilization, a mere

intruder, in his original domain—and under such circumstances only, does he become an object of rough
sport, the incidents of which deserve a passing notice.

The extreme southern portions of the United States
are exceedingly favorable to the growth of the alligator :
in the swamps that stretch over a vast extent of country, inaccessible almost to man, they increase in numbers and size, live undisputed monarchs of their abodes,
exhibiting but little more intelligence, and exerting but
little more volition than decayed trunks of trees, for
which they are not unfrequently mistaken.

In these swampy regions, however, are found high
ridges of land inviting cultivation.   The log cabin takes
the place of the rank vegetation—the evidences of thrift
appear—and as the running streams display themselves,
and are cleared for navigation, that old settler, the alligator, becomes exposed, and falls a victim to the rapacity of man.

Thus hunted—like creatures of higher organization,
he grows more intelligent, from the dangers of his situation ; his instincts become more subtle, and he wars in
turn upon his only enemy ; soon acquires a civilized taste
for pork and poultry, and acquires also a very uncivil-
ized one for dogs.

An alligator, in the truly savage state, is a very
happy reptile : encased in an armor as impenetrable as
that of Ajax, he moves about, unharmed by surrounding circumstances.

'The fangs of the rattlesnake grate over his scales as they would over a file; the constrictor finds nothing about him to crush; the poisonous moccason bites at him in vain; and the greatest pest of all, the mosquito, which fills the air of his abode with a million stings, that burn the flesh of other living things like sparks of fire, buzz out their fury upon his carcass in vain.

To say that he enjoys not these advantages—that he crawls not forth as a proud knight in his armor—that he treads not upon the land as a master—and moves in the water the same—would be doing injustice to his actions, and his habits, and the philosophical example of independence which he sets to the trembling victims daily sacrificed to his wants.

The character of an alligator's face is far from being a flattering letter of recommendation. The mouth is enormously large, and extends from the extreme tip of the nose backwards until it passes the ears; indeed, about one third of the whole animal is mouth, which, being ornamented with superabundant rows of white teeth, gives the same hope of getting out of it, sound in body and mind, if once in, as does the hopper of a bark-mill. Its body is short and round, not unlike that of a horse; its tail is very long, and flattened at the end like an oar. It has the most dexterous use of this appendage, which propels it along swiftly in the water, and on land answers the purpose of a weapon of defence.

The traveller through the lonely swamp at nightfall

often finds himself surrounded by these singular creatures, and if he be unaccustomed to their presence and
habits, they cause great alarm. Scattered about in
every direction, yet hidden by the darkness, he hears
their huge jaws open and shut with a force that makes
a noise, when numbers are congregated, like echoing
thunder.

Again, in the glare of the camp fire will sometimes
be seen the huge alligator crawling within the lighted
circle, attracted by the smell of food—perchance you
have *squatted* upon a nest of eggs, encased with great
judgment in the centre of some high ground you yourself have chosen to pass the night upon.

Many there are who go unconcernedly to sleep with
such intruders in their immediate vicinity; but a rifle
ball, effectively fired, will most certainly leave you unmolested, while the alligator, in its agonies of death, no
doubt takes comfort in the thought, that the sun will
hatch out its eggs, and that there will grow up a numerous brood of young, as hideous and destructive as
itself.

The alligator is a luxurious animal, fond of all the
comforts of life, which are, according to its habits, plentifully scattered around it. We have watched them, enjoying their evening nap in the shades of tangled vine,
and in the hollow trunk of the cypress, or floating like a
log on the top of some sluggish pool.

We have seen them sporting in the green slime, and

watching, like a dainty gourmand, the fattest frogs and longest snakes; but they are in the height of their glory, stretched out upon the sand-bar in the meridian sun, when the summer heats pour down and radiate back from the parched sand, as tangibly as they would from red-hot iron. In such places will they bask, and blow off, with a loud noise, the inflated air and water which expands within them, occasionally rolling about their swinish eyes with a slowness of motion, which, while it expresses the most perfect satisfaction, is in no way calculated to agitate their nerves, or discompose them, by too suddenly taking the impression of outward objects.

While thus disposed, and after the first nap is taken, they amuse themselves with opening their huge jaws to their widest extent, upon the inside of which, instinctively settle, thousands of mosquitoes and other noxious insects which infest the abode of the alligator. When the inside of the mouth is thus covered, the reptile brings his jaws together with inconceivable velocity, gives a gulp or two, and again sets his formidable trap for this small game.

Some years since, a gentleman in the southern part of Louisiana, on "opening a plantation," found, after most of the forest trees had been cleared off, that in the centre of his land was a boggy piece of low soil, nearly twenty acres in extent. This place was singularly infested with alligators. Among the first victims that fell a prey to their rapacity, were a number of hogs and fine poultry;

next followed, nearly all of a pack of fine deer hounds. It may be easily imagined that the last outrage was not passed over with indifference. The leisure time of every day was devoted to their extermination, until the cold of winter rendered them torpid, and buried them up in the earth.

The following summer, as is naturally the case, the swamp, from the intense heat, contracted in its dimensions; a number of artificial ditches drained off the water, and left the alligators little else to live in than mud, which was about the consistency of good mortar: still the alligators clung with singular tenacity to their native homesteads, as if perfectly conscious that the coming fall would bring them rain. While thus exposed, a general attack was planned and carried into execution, and nearly every alligator was destroyed. It was a fearful and disgusting sight to see them rolling about in the thick sediment, striking their immense jaws together in the agony of death.

Dreadful to relate, the stench of these decaying bodies in the hot sun, soon produced an unthought-of evil. Teams of oxen were used in vain to haul them away; the progress of corruption under the influence of a tropical climate made the attempt fruitless.

On the very edge of the swamp, with nothing exposed but the head, lay one huge monster, evidently sixteen or eighteen feet long; he had been wounded in the melée, and made incapable of moving, and the heat had actually baked the earth around his body as firmly as if he was imbedded in cement. It was a cruel and singular exhibition to see so much power and destructiveness so helpless.

We amused ourselves in throwing various things into his great cavernous mouth, which he would grind up between his teeth. Seizing a large oak rail, we attempted to run it down his throat, but it was impossible; for he held it for a moment as firmly as if it had been the bow of a ship, then with his jaws crushed and ground it to fine splinters.

The old fellow, however, had his revenge; the dead alligators were found more destructive than the living ones, and the plantation for a season had to be abandoned.

In shooting the alligator, the bullet must hit just in front of the fore legs, where the skin is most vulnerable; it seldom penetrates in other parts of the body.

Certainty of aim, therefore, tells in alligator shooting, as it does in every thing else connected with sporting.

Generally, the alligator, when wounded, retreats to some obscure place; but if wounded in a *bayou*, where the banks are steep, and not affording any hiding-places, he makes considerable amusement in his convolutions in the water, and in his efforts to avoid the pain of his smarting wounds.

In shooting, the instant that you fire, the reptile

disappears, and you are for a few moments unable to learn the extent of injury you have inflicted.

An excellent shot, who sent the load with almost unerring certainty through the eye, made one at a huge alligator, and, as usual, he disappeared, but almost instantly rose again, spouting water from his nose, not unlike a whale. A second ball, shot in his tail, sent him down again, but he instantly rose and spouted: this singular conduct prompted a bit of provocation, in the way of a plentiful sprinkling of bits of wood, rattled against his hide. The alligator lashed himself into a fury; the blood started from his mouth; he beat the water with his tail until he covered himself with spray, but never sunk without instantly rising again.

In the course of the day he died and floated ashore; and, on examination, it was found that the little valve with which nature has provided the reptile, to close over its nostrils when under water, had been cut off by the first shot, and he was thus compelled to stay on the top of the water to keep from being drowned.

We have heard of many since who have tried thus to wound them, and although they have been hit in the nose, yet they have been so crippled as to sink and die.

The alligator, when inhabiting places near plantations, is particularly destructive on pigs and dogs, and if you wish to shoot them, you can never fail to draw them on the surface of the water, if you will make a dog yell, or a pig squeal; and that too, in places where you may have been fishing all day, without suspecting their presence.

Herodotus mentions the catching of crocodiles in the Nile, by baiting a hook with flesh, and then attracting the reptile towards it by making a hog squeal.

The ancient Egyptian manner of killing the crocodile is different from that of the present day, as powder and ball have changed the manner of destruction; but the fondness for pigs in the crocodile and alligator, for more than two thousand years, remains the same.

BUFFALO HUNTING.

THE buffalo is decidedly one of the noblest victims that is sacrificed to the ardor of the sportsman. There is a massiveness about his form, and a magnificence associated with his home, that give him a peculiar interest.

No part of North America was originally unoccupied by the buffalo. The places where now are cities and towns, are remembered as their haunts; but they have kept with melancholy strides before the "march of civilization," and now find a home, daily more exposed and invaded, only on that division of our continent west of the Mississippi.

But in the immense wilds that give birth to the waters of the Missouri—on the vast prairies that stretch out like inland seas between the "great lakes" and the Pacific, and extend towards the tropics until they touch the foot of the Cordilleras, the buffalo roams still wild and free.

But the day of his glory is past. The Anglo-Saxon,

more wanton of place than the savage himself, possessed
of invincible courage and unlimited resources, and feeling adventure a part of life itself, has already penetrated
the remotest fastnesses, and wandered over the most extended plains.   Where the live lightning leaps from
rock to rock, opening yawning caverns to the dilating
eye, or spends its fury upon the desert, making it a
sheet of fire, there have been his footsteps ; and there
has the buffalo smarted beneath his prowess, and kissed
the earth.

The child of fortune from the " old world," the favorite of courts, has abandoned his home and affectations,
and sought, among these western wilds, the enjoyment
of nature in her own loveliness.   The American hunter
frolics over them as a boy enjoying his Saturday sport.
The Indian—like his fathers, ever restless—scours the
mountain and the plain ; and men of whatever condition
here meet *equal, as sportsmen;* and their great feats of
honor and of arms, are at the sacrifice of the buffalo.

In their appearance, the buffalos present a singular
mixture of the ferocious and comical.   At a first glance
they excite mirth ; they appear to be the sleck-blooded
kine, so familiar to the farmyard, but muffled about the
shoulders in a coarse shawl, and wearing a mask and
beard, as if in some outlandish disguise.

Their motions, too, are novel.   They dash off, tail
up, shaking their great woolly heads, and planting their
feet under them, with a swinging gait and grotesque pre-

cision, that suggests the notion that they are a jolly set of dare-devils, fond of fun and extravagances, and disposed to have their jokes at the expense of all dignity of carriage, and the good opinion of the grave portion of the world.

But, upon nearer examination, you quail before the deep destructive instinct expressed in the eye; the shaggy mane distends, and shows the working of muscles fairly radiant with power; the fore foot dashes into and furrows the hard turf; the tail waves in angry curves; the eyeballs fill with blood, and with bellowing noise that echoes like the thunder, the white foam covers the shaggy jaws. Then the huge form before you grows into a mountain, then is exhibited an animal sublimity, a world of appetite without thought, and force without reason.

Standing on one of the immense prairies of the " south-west," you look out upon what seems to be the green waving swell of the sea, suddenly congealed—and it requires but little fancy to imagine, when the storm-cloud sweeps over it, and the rain dashes in torrents, and the fierce winds bear down upon it, that the magic that holds it immovable, may be broken, and leave you helpless on the billowy wave.

On such an expanse, sublime from its immensity, roams the buffalo, in numbers commensurate with the extent, and not unfrequently covering the landscape, until their diminishing forms mingle in the opposite horizons, like mocking spectres. Such is the arena of sport, and such in quantity, is the game.

To the wild Indian, the buffalo hunt awakens the soul as absorbingly as does the defying yell on the war-path. With inflated nostril and distended eye, he dashes after his victim, revelling in the fruition of all the best hopes of his existence, and growing in the conceit of his favor with the " Great Spirit."

To the rude, white hunter, less imaginative than the savage ; the buffalo hunt is the high consummation of his propensity and power to destroy. It gratifies his ambition, and feasts his appetite ; his work is tangible ; he feels—hears—tastes—and sees it ; it is the very unloosing of all the rough passions of our nature, with the conscience entirely at rest.

To the " sportsman," who is matured in the constraint of cities, and in the artificial modes of enlightened society, and who retains within his bosom the leaven of our coarser nature, the buffalo hunt stirs up the latent fires repressed by a whole life ; they break out with ardor, and he enters into the chase with an abandonment, which, while it gratifies every animal sense possessed by the savage and hunter, opens a thousand other avenues of high enjoyment, known only to the cultivated and refined mind.

Among the Indians there are but few methods of hunting the buffalo ; yet there are tribes who display more skill than others, and seem to bring more intellect

to bear in the sport.   The Comanches in the south, and
the Sioux in the north, are, from their numbers, warlike
character, and wealth, by the aborigines, considered as
the *true buffalo hunters.*

The Comanches inhabit one of the loveliest countries
in the world for a winter home—but when the heats of
summer drive them northward, they travel over the
loveliest herbage, variegated by a thousand perfumed
flowers, that yield fragrance under every crush of the
foot.   The wide savannas, that are washed by the
Trinity and Brasos rivers, are every where variegated
with clumps of live-oak trees, among which you involun-
tarily look for the mansion of some feudal lord.

Here are realized almost the wildest dreams of the
future to the red men ; and here the Comanches, strong
in numbers, and rich in the spontaneous productions of
their native land, walk proud masters, and exhibit savage life in some of the illusive charms we throw around
it while bringing a refined imagination to view such life
in the distance.

Thousands of this tribe of Indians will sometimes be
engaged at one time in a buffalo hunt.   In their wanderings about the prairies, they leave trails worn like a
long-travelled road.   Following the " scouts," until the
vicinity of the animal is proclaimed, and then selecting
a halting-place, favorable both for fuel and water, the
ceremonies preparatory to a grand hunt take place.

Then are commenced, with due solemnity, the

prayers of the priests. A solemn feeling pervades every thoughtful member of the tribe. · The death-defying warrior, who curls his scalp-lock derisively when he thinks of his enemies, now bows in submission to the invisible presence that bestows upon the red man the great game he is about to destroy, and it is not until the fastings, prayers, and self-sacrifices are finished that the excitement of the chase commences.

The morning sun greets the hunter divested of all unnecessary clothing, *his arrows numbered*—his harness in order—a plume floats from his crown—his long hair streams down his back—his well-trained horse, as wild as himself, anticipates the sport, and paws with impatience the ground.

Far, far in the horizon are moving about, in black masses, the game; and with an exulting whoop, a party start off *with the wind*, dash across the prairie, and are soon out of sight.

The buffalo is a wary animal; unwieldy as he appears, his motions are quick, and, at the approach of a human being, he instinctively takes the alarm, and flies.

An hour or two may elapse, when the distant masses of buffalo begin to move. There is evident alarm spreading through the ranks. Suddenly they fly!

Then it is that thousands of fleet and impatient horsemen, like messengers of the wind, dash off *and meet the herds*. The party first sent out are pressing them in the rear; confusion seizes upon the alarmed animals, and they scatter in every direction over the plain. Now the hunters select their victims, and the blood is up. On speeds the Indian and his horse. The long mane mingles with the light garments of the rider, and both seem instigated by the same instinct and spirit. On plunges the unwieldy object of pursuit, shaking his shaggy head, as if in despair of his safety. The speed of the horse soon overtakes the buffalo.

The rider, dropping his rein, plucks an arrow from his quiver, presses his knees to the horse's sides, draws his bow, and with unerring aim, drives the delicate shaft into the vitals of the huge animal, who rushes on a few yards, curls his tail upwards, falters, falls on his face, and dies. An exulting shout announces the success, and the warrior starts off after another; and if he has performed his task well, *every bow that has twanged,* marks the ownership of a huge carcass upon the sea of the prairie, as sacredly as the waiffe of the whaleman his victim on the sea itself.

Thus, when the day's sport is over, every arrow is returned to its owner. If two have been used to kill the same animal, or any are wanting, having been carried away in mere flesh wounds; the want of skill is upbraided, and the unfortunate hunter shrinks from the sarcasms and observation of the successful, with shame.

Following the hunter are the women, the laborers of the tribe. To them is allotted the task of tearing off the skin, selecting the choice pieces of flesh, and preserving what is not immediately consumed.

Then follows the great feast. The Indian gluts himself with marrow and fatness, his eyes, lately so bright with the fire of sport, are now glazed with bestiality, and he spends days and nights in wasteful extravagance, trusting to the abundance of nature to supply the wants of the future.

Such are the general characteristics of the buffalo hunt; and the view applies with equal truth to all the different tribes who pursue, as a distinct and powerful people—this noble game.

An Indian armed for the buffalo hunt, and his horse, form two of the most romantic and picturesque of beings. The loose garment that he wears is beautifully arranged about his person, disclosing the muscles of the shoulder and chest. Across his back is slung his quiver of arrows, made from the skin of some wild animal; his long bow, slightly arched by the sinewy string, is used gracefully as a rest for his extended arm.

The horse, with a fiery eye—a mane that waves over his front like drapery, and falls in rakish masses across his wide forehead—a sweeping tail ornamented with the brilliant plumage of tropical birds; champs on his rude bit, and arches his neck with impatience, as the scent of the game reaches his senses. Frequently will these graceful Apollos pass before you, bounding gracefully along, and more than rivalling the beauty, of the equestrians portrayed upon the Elgin marbles.

Then there may be seen dashing off with incredible swiftness, a living representation of the centaur;—and as one of these wild horses and wilder men, viewed from below, stand in broad relief against the clear sky, you see an equestrian statue that art has never equalled.

The exultation of such a warrior, in the excitement of a buffalo hunt, rings in silvery tones across the plain, as if in his lungs was the music of a " well-chosen pack ; " the huge victims of pursuit, as they hear it, impel onwards with redoubled speed,—they feel that a hurricane of death is in the cry.

Take a hunting-party of fifty " warriors," starting on a buffalo hunt. Imagine a splendid fall morning in the southern part of the buffalo " grounds."

The sun rises over the prairie, like a huge illuminated ball; it struggles on through the mists, growing gradually brighter in its ascent, breaking its way into the clear atmosphere in long-reaching rays, dispelling the mists in wreathing columns, and starting up currents of air to move them sportively about; slowly they ascend and are lost in the ether above.

You discover before you, and under you, a rich and beautifully variegated carpet, enamelled by a thousand flowers, glistening with the pearly drops of dew, as the horizontal rays of the sun reach them.

Here and there are plants of higher growth, as if

9*

some choice garden had been stripped of its inclosures : shrubbery waves the pendant blossom, and wastes a world of sweetness on the desert air. Among these flowery coverts browse the graceful deer and antelope.

Far before you are the long dark lines of the buffalo. In the centre of the group feed the cows and calves. Upon the outside are the sturdy bulls : some with their mouths to the ground, are making it shake with their rough roar ; others sportively tear up the turf with their horns ; others not less playful, rush upon each other's horns with a force that sends them reeling on their sides.

Animal enjoyment seems rife, and as they turn their nostrils upwards and snuff in the balmy air and greet the warm sun, they little dream that around them are circling the wild Indian, wilder—more savage—and more wary, than themselves.

Fancy these Indians prompted by all the habits and feelings of the hunter and warrior, mingling with the sport the desire to distinguish themselves, as on a field of honor, little less only in importance than the war-path. With characters of high repute to sustain, or injured reputations to build up—of victory for the ear of love —of jealousy—of base passions—and a thirst of blood, and you will have some idea of the promptings of the hearts of those about to engage in the chase.

The time arrives. The parties already out, are driving the herd towards the starting-place of the warriors.

They have sent up their war-cry in one united whoop, which has startled the feeding monsters, as if the lightning had fallen among them. With a bellowing response the buffalo shake their heads, and simultaneously start off.

The fearful whoop meets them at every point. Confusion seizes upon the herd. The sport has begun.

In every direction you see the unequal chase; the Indians seem multiplied into hundreds; the plain becomes dotted over with the dying animals, and the whoop rings in continuous shouts upon the air, as if the fiends themselves were loose.

Now you see a single warrior: before him is rushing a buffalo, which shows from his immense size, that he is one of the masters of the herd; his pursuer is a veteran hunter, known far and near for his prowess.

Yonder go some twenty buffalos of every size, pursued by three or four tyros, who yet know not the art of separating their victim from the herd.

Yonder goes a bull, twice shot at, yet only wounded in the flesh—some one will have to gather wood with the women for his want of skill.

There goes an old chief: his leggins are trimmed with the hair of twenty scalps, taken from the heads of the very Indians on whose grounds he was hunting buffalo; he is a great warrior; he sings, that his bow unbent is a great tree, which he alone can bend. See the naked arm, and the rigid muscles, as he draws the arrow to the *very head :* the bull vomits blood and falls : beyond him on the grass is the arrow; it passes through, where a rifle ball would have stopped and flattened ere it had made half the journey.

Here are two buffalo bulls side by side; they make the earth tremble by their measured tread; their sides are reeking with sweat. Already have they been singled out. Approaching them are two horsemen; upon the head of one glistens the silvery hair of age; the small leggins also betray the old man : the other is just entering the prime of life; every thing about him is sound, full, and sleek. The old man compresses his mouth into a mere line; the eye is open and steady as a basilisk; the skin inanimate. The eyes of the young man dance with excitement, the blood flows quickly through the dark skin; and gives a feverish look to his lip and cheek. What a tale is told in these differences of look ! how one seems reaching into the future, and the other going back to the past !

He of the flushed cheek touches his quiver, the bow is bent, the arrow speeds its way and penetrates its victim. The old man—he too takes an arrow, slowly he places it across his bow, then bending it as if to make its ends meet, he leans forward—sends the arrow home —the bull falls, while the one first wounded pursues his way. The old man gives a taunting shout as a token of his success.

The young warrior, confused by his want of skill,

and alarmed lest his aged rival should complete the work he so bunglingly began, unguardedly presses too near the bull, who, smarting with his wound, turns upon his heels, and, with one mad plunge, tears out the bowels of the steed, and rolls him and rider on the turf. He next rushes at the rider.

The Indian, wary as the panther, springs aside, and the bull falls headlong on the ground. Ere the bull recovers himself, the bow is again bent, the flint-headed arrow strikes the hard rib, splits it asunder, and enters the heart.

The old warrior has looked on with glazed eye and expressionless face, and the young man feels that he has added no laurels to his brow, for an arrow has been spent in vain and his steed killed under him.

There goes a " brave " with a bow by his side, and his right hand unoccupied. He presses his horse against the very sides of the animal which he is pursuing. Now he leans forward until he seems hidden between the buffalo and his horse. He rises; a gory arrow is in his hand; he has plucked it from a " flesh wound " at full speed, and while in luck, has with better aim brought his victim to the earth.

The sun is now fairly in its zenith : the buffalos that have escaped are hurrying away, with a speed that will soon carry them miles beyond the hunter's pursuit.

The Indians are coming in from the field. The horses breathe hard and are covered with foam. The faces of the Indians are still lit up with excitement, that will soon pass away, and leave them cold and expression-less. The successful hunters spare not the gibe and joke at the expense of the unfortunate. Slowly they wend their way back to " the encampment ; " their work is done.

The squaws, who, like vultures, follow on in the rear, eagerly begin their disgusting work. The maiden is not among them ; slavery commences only with married life ; but the old, the wrinkled, the viragoes and vixens, tear off the skins, jerk the meat, gather together the marrow bones, and the humps, the tongues, and the paunch ; and before the sun has fairly set, they are in the camp with the rewards of the day's hunt.

The plain, so beautiful in the morning, is scattered over with carcasses already offensive with decay ; the grass is torn up, the flowers destroyed ; and the wolf and buzzard and the carrion crow are disputing for the loathsome meal, while their already gorged appetites seem bursting with repletion.

As might be supposed, the members of a party of adventurers once accustomed to the luxuries of refined life, and who had recently for weeks slept in the open air, congratulated themselves when they discovered upon the distant horizon the signs that mark the habita-tion of a " squatter." A thousand recollections of the comforts of civilized life pressed upon us before we reached the abode. We speculated upon the rich treat of delicacies which we should enjoy, but a near inspection at once dispelled our illusions.

On the confines of the buffalo hunting-grounds, had settled a family, consisting of a strange mixture of enterprise and idleness, of ragged-looking men and homely women. They seemed to have all the bad habits of the Indians, with none of their redeeming qualities. They were willing to live without labor, and subsist upon the precarious bounties of nature.

Located in the fine climate of Northern Texas, the whole year was to them little less than a continued spring, and the abundance of game with which they were surrounded afforded, what seemed to them, all the comforts of life. The men never exerted themselves except when hunger prompted, or a spent magazine made the acquisition of "peltries" necessary to barter for powder and ball.

A more lazy, contemptible set of creatures never existed, and we would long since have forgotten them, had not our introduction to them associated itself with *our first buffalo steak.*

A large rudely-constructed shed, boarded up on the northern side, was the abode. Upon close examination it appeared that this "shed" was the common dwelling-place of the "family," which consisted not only of the human beings, but also of horses, cows, goats, and ill-bred poultry.

Immediately around the caravansera, the prairie

grass struggled for a sickly growth.   As you entered it, you found yourself growing deeper and deeper in a fine dust, that had, in the course of time, been worked out of the soil.   Some coarse blankets were suspended through the enclosure, as retiring rooms for the women. On the ground were strewn buffalo skins, from which the animal inhabitants alone kept aloof.

We entered without seeing a human being.   After some delay, however, a little nondescript, with a white sunburnt head, thrust aside the blankets, and hallooed out, " They ain't injuns."   The mother then showed herself.   She was as far removed from feminine as pos-sible, and appeared as unmoved at our presence as the post that sustained the roof of her house.

We asked for lodging and food ; she nodded a cold assent and disappeared.   Not disposed to be fastidious, we endeavored to make ourselves as comfortable as pos-sible, and wait for the development of coming events.

In the course of an hour a woman younger than the first made her appearance, and on hearing the detail of our wants, she wrinkled her soiled visage into a distort-ed smile, and told us that the " men " would soon be home with " buffalo meat," and then our wants should be supplied.

Whatever might have been our disappointment at what we saw around us, the name of buffalo meat dis-pelled it all.   The great era in our frontier wanderings was about to commence, and with smiles from our party that for expression would have done credit to rival belles, we lounged upon the skins upon the ground.

It is needless for us to say what were our ideas of the "men," soon to make their appearance. Buffalo hunters were, of course, tall, fine-looking fellows—active as cats—mounted upon wild steeds—armed with terrible rifles, and all the paraphernalia of the hunter's art.

The Dutch angels, that figure so conspicuously on many a gem of art in the "Lowlands," are certainly not farther removed from the beautiful creations of Milton, than were the buffalo hunters that we saw from the standard our imagination and reading had conjured up.

Two short, ill-formed men finally appeared, whose bow-legs, formidable shocks of red hair, clothes of skin, and shuffling gaits, were the realities of our poetical conceptions.

Whatever might have been the charms of their faces, our admiration was absorbed in viewing their nether garments. They were made of undressed deer-skin, the hair worn outside. When first made, they were evidently of the length of pantaloons, but the drying qualities of the sun had, in course of time, no doubt imperceptibly to the wearers, shortened them into the dignity of breeches. To see these worthies standing up was beyond comparison ridiculous. They seemed to have had immense pommels fastened to their knees and seats.

Under other circumstances, the tailor craft of the frontier would have elicited great merriment ; but a starving stomach destroys jokes. Courtesies suitable were exchanged, and the preliminaries for a hearty meal agreed upon, the basis of which was to be, *buffalo steaks.*

A real buffalo steak! eaten in the very grounds which the animal inhabits! What romance! what a diploma of a sportsman's enterprise!

Whatever might have been my disappointment in the hunters, I knew that meat was meat, and that the immutable laws of nature would not fail, though my ideas of the romantic in men were entirely disappointed. A promise that our wants should soon be supplied, brought us to that unpleasant time, in every-day life, which prefaces an expected and wished-for meal.

Seated, like barbarians, upon the floor, myself and companions enjoyed the pleasing mental operation of calculating how little the frontier family we were visiting were worth, for any moral quality; and the physical exercise of keeping off, as much as possible, thousands of fleas, and other noxious insects, that infested the dust in which we sat.

While thus disposed of, the "hunters" were busy in various ways about the premises, and received from us the elegant names of "Bags" and "Breeches," from some fancied or real difference in their inexpressibles. "Breeches," who was evidently the business man, came near where we were sitting, and threw down upon the ground, what appeared, at a superficial glance, to be an enormous pair of saddle-bags. He then asked his companion-in-arms for a knife, to cut for the strangers some buffalo steaks.

Now if the nondescript before me had as coolly proposed to cut steaks from an ill-natured cur that was wistfully eyeing the saddle-bags, no more surprise could have been exhibited by my companions than was, when they heard the suggestion.

The knife was brought, and " Breeches " made an essay at cutting up the saddle-bags, which gave him, dressed as he was in skins, the appearance of a wild robber just about to search the effects of some murdered traveller. The work progressed bravely, and, to our surprise, soon were exhibited crude slices of meat. What we saw were the fleshy parts of a buffalo's hams, ingeniously connected together by the skin that passed over the back of the animal, and so dissected from the huge frame as to enable it easily to be carried on a horse, and thus brought " into camp."

As the sounds that accompany the frying of meat saluted our ears, we moved into the open air, to avoid the certain knowledge that we were about to complete the eating of that peck of dirt, said to be necessary before we die. Before the door were the two horses belonging to our hosts; just as they returned from the hunt, and upon one still hung huge pieces of meat, thus simply, and frontier-like, held together for transportation.

Our first buffalo steak disappointed us. The romance of months—and of years—was sadly broken in upon. The squalid wretchedness of those who administered to our wants, made rebellious even our hungry stomachs; and we spent our first night of real disappointment on the great prairies, under circumstances which we thought, before our sad experience, would have afforded us all the substantial food for body and mind that we could have desired.

SCENES IN BUFFALO HUNTING.

THE morning following the adventure with the steak, found our little party rifles in hand, and bent upon a buffalo hunt. The animals, it would seem, for the especial benefit of " Breeches " and " Bags," had come " lower down " than usual, and we were among the buffalo much sooner than we expected to be.

So far, fortune favored us; and a gayer party never set out on a frolic, than followed the deer-skin inexpressibles on the fine December morning to which we have alluded.

As we jaunted along, crushing a thousand wild flowers under our horses' feet, the deer would bound like visions of grace and beauty from our presence; but we essayed not such small game. Our ideas and nostrils, expanded by the associations around us; we grew merry at the thought of killing bucks, turkeys, and other *helpless*, *little* game, and laughed so loudly, at the conceit of drawing a deadly weapon upon a thing as small as a woodcock, that the wild, half devil, and half Indian horses on which we were mounted, pricked up their ears and tails, as if they expected that the next salute would be the war-whoop and a fight.

Ahead of us we beheld the buzzards, circling in groups, whirling down in aerial flights to the earth, as if busy with their prey. We passed them at their gross repast over a mountain of meat, which had, the day before, been full of life and fire, but had fallen under the visitation of our guides and scarecrows; and provided the very steaks that had met with so little affection from our appetites. Soon we discovered signs of immediate vicinity of the buffalo, and on a little examination from the top of a "swell of land," we saw them feeding off towards the horizon, like vast herds of cattle quietly grazing within the inclosure of the farm-yard.

As distant as they were, our hearts throbbed violently as we contemplated the sanguinary warfare we were about to engage in, and the waste of life that would ensue.

Still, we were impelled on by an irresistible and overpowering instinct to begin the hunt.

"Breeches" and "Bags" carried over their shoulders poles about six feet long; but as they were destitute of any visible spear, we looked upon them as inoffensive weapons, and concluded that they had come out just to act as guides. In fact, we could not imagine that such wretched-looking fellows, so badly mounted, could hunt any thing.

For ourselves, we were armed with the terrible rifle ; and so satisfied were we of its prowess, that we thought the very appearance of its muzzle more deadly than the demonstrated use of all other weapons beside.

Keeping to the windward of the buffalo, we skirted round until we got them between us and the shed wherein we passed the night.

Then the signal was given, and in a pell-mell manner we charged on, every man for himself. We approached within a quarter of a mile before the herd took the alarm.

Then, smelling us on the air, they turned their noses towards the zenith, gave a sort of rough snort, and broke simultaneously off at a full gallop. As soon as this noise was heard by our horses, they increased their speed, and entered into the sport as ardently as their riders.

The rough beasts rode by "Bags" and "Breeches" did wonders, and seemed really to fly, while their riders poised themselves gallantly, carrying their long poles in front of them with a grace, from the excitement of the moment, that would have honored a Cossack bearing his spear.

The buffalo, with their tails high in the air, ran close together, rattling their horns singularly loud ; while the horses, used to the chase, endeavored to separate a single object for especial pursuit.

This once accomplished, it was easy to range alongside; and in this situation the members of our party severally found themselves; and drawing deadly aim, as they supposed, the crack of the sharp rifle was heard over the prairies, and yet nothing was brought to the ground. Contrary to all this, a noble bull lay helpless in the very track I took, the fruit of "Breeches'" murderous skill; and from the energetic manner with which he pressed on, we became satisfied that there was a magic in those sticks we had not dreamed of.

Our curiosity excited, we ran across the diameter of a circle he was forming, and came by his side. Soon he overtook his object of pursuit, and thrusting forward his pole, we saw glittering, for the first time, on its end a short blade; a successful thrust *severed the hamstring*, and a mountain of flesh and life fell helpless on the prairie. The thing was done so suddenly, that some moments elapsed before we could overcome our astonishment. My horse approached the animal, and thrusting forward his head and ears, snorted in his face, and then commenced quietly cropping the grass.

It would be impossible for me to describe my emotions as I, dismounting, examined the gigantic and wounded bull before me. There he lay—an animal, that from his singular expression of face and general appearance, joined with his immense size, looked like some animated specimen of the monsters of the antediluvian world.

Rising on his fore legs, he shook his mane and beard in defiance, and flashed from his eyes an unconquerable determination terrible to behold.

Gazing upwards, we beheld, fearfully caricatured, the shaggy trappings of the lion, and the wild fierceness of a perfect savage, the whole rising above us in huge unwieldy proportions. He made no demonstration of attack, his usual expression of defiance had changed into that of seeming regret and heartsick pain; his small bright eye roamed over the beautiful prairie, and watched the retreating herds of his fellows, as would an old patriarch when about to bid adieu to the world; and as the dying creature gazed on, the tear struggled in his eye, rolled over the rough sunburnt hair, dashed like a bright jewel from his knotted beard, and fell to the ground.

This exhibition of suffering nature cooled the warm blood of the hunt within me; the instinct of destruction was, for the time, overpowered by that of better feelings, and could we have restored to health the wounded animal, it would have given us a thrill of real pleasure to have seen him again free, and bounding over the plain.

Instead of this, we took from our belt a pistol, called upon mercy to sanction our deed, and sent the cold lead through the thoughtful eye into the brain: the body sank upon its knees, in ready acknowledgment of the power of man; the heavy head plunged awkwardly to the ground; a tremulous motion passed through the frame—and the wild monarch was dead.

The momentary seriousness of my own feelings, occasioned by the incidents above related, was broken in upon by a loud exulting whoop, prolonged into a quavering sound, such as will sometimes follow a loud blast of a trumpet at the mouth of an expert player.

It was a joyous whoop, and vibrated through our hearts—we looked up, and saw just before us a young Indian warrior, mounted upon a splendid charger, and rushing across the plain, evidently in pursuit of the retreating buffalo.

As he swept by, he threw himself forward in his saddle, and placed his right hand over his eyes, as if to shade them from the sun, making a picture of the most graceful and eager interest.

His horse carried his head low down, running like a rabbit, while the long flowing mane waved in the wind like silk. Horse and rider were almost equally undressed; both wiry; and every muscle, as it came into action, gave evidence of youth and power. Over the horse's head, and inwrought in the hair of the tail, streamed plumes plucked from the gay flamingo. Every thing was life—moving, dashing life—gay as the sunshine that glistens on the rippling wave where the falcon wets his wing.

This soul-stirring exhibition warmed us into action,

and, mounting our horses, we dashed after the red man. Our direction soon brought us in sight of the retreating buffalo ; and, with the Indian and myself, dashed on a third person, the valiant " Breeches."

I followed as a spectator, and keeping close to both, was enabled to watch two beings so widely different in form, looks, and action, while bent on the same exciting pursuit.

Fortunately, two buffalos of large size, cut off from the main body, were being driven towards us by some one of our party : a distant report of a rifle, and the sudden stopping of one of the animals, told the tale.

The remaining bull, alarmed by the report of the rifle, rushed madly on, with enemies in front and rear. Discovering its new danger, it wheeled almost on its heels and ran for life. Whatever might have been our vivid imaginings of the excitement of a buffalo chase, we now felt the fruition beyond our most sanguine hopes.

Before us ran the buffalo, then followed the Indian, and beside him " Breeches," so closely that you would have thought a dark Apollo on a mettled charger, had by some necromancy cast the shadow of a cornfield scarecrow. We soon gained on the buffalo, rapidly as he moved his feet under him. " Breeches " poised his rude instrument to make the fearful cut at the hamstrings, when the Indian, plucking an arrow from his quiver, bent his bow, and pointing it at " Breeches' " side,

——, let it fly. The stick held by " Breeches "
leaped from his grasp as if it had been struck by a club ;
another instant, and again the bow was bent ; guiding
his horse with his feet, the Indian came alongside of the
buffalo, and drove the arrow to the feather into his
side.

A chuckling guttural laugh followed this brilliant
exploit, and as the animal, after a few desperate leaps,
fell forward and vomited blood, again was repeated the
same joyous whoop that so roused our stagnant blood at
the beginning of the chase.

The instant that " Breeches " dropped his stick, his
horse, probably from habit, stopped ; and the one on
which I rode followed the example. The Indian dis-
mounted, and stood beside the buffalo the instant he fell.
The shaggy and rough appearance of the dead animal—
the healthy-looking and ungroomed horse with his roving
eye and long mane—and the Indian himself, contem-
plating his work like some bronze statue of antique art
—formed a group, the simplicity and beautiful wildness
of which would have struck the eye of the most insensible.

" Breeches," alike insensible to the charms of the
tailor's art, and to the picturesque—handed the Indian
his first fired arrow, and then stooping down, with a
gentle pressure, thrust the head of the one in the buffalo through the opposite side from which it entered,
and handed it to its owner, with disgust marked upon

"There was a simplicity and beautiful wildness about the group, that would have struck the eye of the most insensible."—*page* 220.

his face, that displayed no great pleasure at the Indian's appearance and company.

Among the Indian tribes there are certain styles of doing things, which are as essential to command the attention and win the favor of a real hunter, as there are peculiar manners and modes commended, and only acknowledged, by sportsmen.

A poor despicable tribe, bearing the name of Ta-wa-ki-na, inhabiting the plains of Texas, kill the buffalo by hamstringing them, and are, therefore, despised and driven out from among the " Indian men."

A young Comanche chief, fond of adventure, and friendly with " Breeches," had gone out of his way to join in our sport; and having shown to the white man his skill, and for " Breeches " his contempt for his imitations of a despised tribe, he passed on in pursuit of his own business, either of war or of pleasure.

The experience of our first buffalo hunt satisfied us that the rifle was not the most effective instrument in destroying the animal. The time consumed in loading the rifle is sufficient for an Indian to shoot several arrows, while the arrow more quickly kills than the bullet.

As the little party to which I was attached had more notions of fun than any particular method of hunting, a day was set apart for a buffalo hunt, " Ta-wa-ki-na fashion," and for this purpose rifles were laid aside, and poles about seven feet long, with razor blades fastened on them a few inches from the end, so as to form a fork, were taken in their place.   Arriving in the vicinity of the buffalo, those who were disposed entered into the sport pell-mell.

Like a faithful squire I kept close at the heels of " Breeches," who soon brought a fine young heifer bellowing to the ground.   As the animal uttered sounds of pain, one or two fierce-looking bulls that gallantly followed in the rear, exposing themselves to attack to preserve the weaker members of the herd, stopped short for an instant, and eyed us with most unpleasant curiosity.   This roused the knight of the deer-skin breeches ; and, brandishing his stick over his head with a remarkable degree of dexterity, he dashed off as if determined to slay both at once.

My two companions who started out as Ta-wa-ki-nas, had done but little execution, not understanding their work, or alarmed at so near an approach of the animals they wounded, without bringing them to the earth.   As " Breeches " dashed on after the bulls, he severally crossed the route of all who were on the chase ; and as he was unquestionably the hero of the day, all followed in his train, determined to see hamstringing done scientifically.

It is a singular fact in the formation of the buffalo, and the familiar cattle of the farm-yard, that, although so much alike in general appearance, the domesticated animal will, after being hamstrung, run long distances.

The buffalo, on the contrary, the moment that the tendon is severed, falls to the ground entirely helpless, and perfectly harmless to one beyond the reach of its horns. A very short chase in company with "Breeches," brought us up to one of the bulls; he poised his stick, thrust it forward, and the *tendon Achilles*, full of life and full of action, was touched by the sharp blade; its tension, as it sustained the immense bull in his upward leaps, made it, when severed, spring back as will the breaking string of the harp; and the helpless beast, writhing in pain, came to the ground.

One of our party on witnessing this exhibition, gave an exulting shout, and declared that he would bring a buffalo down or break his neck; he soon came beside a venerable bull, and as he made repeated thrusts, a thousand directions were given him as to the manner of proceeding. The race was a well contested one, and the heels of the pursued animal were strangely accelerated by the thrusts made at him in his rear.

A lunge was finally accomplished by the "Ta-wa-ki-na," that almost threw him from his horse; the fearful cut brought the huge bull directly under the rider's feet; the next instant the noble steed was impaled upon the buffalo's horns, and the unfortunate rider lay insensible on the ground. In the excitement, the wrong hamstring had been cut, and, as the animal always falls upon the wounded side, the mistake had caused the bull to become a stumbling block in his path.

We hastened to our unfortunate companion, chafed his temples, and brought him to his senses. Happily, save the loss of a generous steed, no great damage was done. The " Ta-wa-ki-na " acknowledged that hamstringing buffalo was as contemptible, as it was thought to be by the Comanche chief. Thus ended this novel and barbarian hunt, which afforded incidents for many rough jokes and amusing reflections on hamstringing buffalos.

As a reward for these frontier sports it is but just to say, that we feasted plentifully upon buffalo steaks, marrow bones, humps, and tongues ; yet surfeited as was the body, the mind was not satisfied.

There was a waste of life and of food accompanying the hunting of the animal, that, like an ever-present spirit of evil, took away from our enjoyment that zest which is necessary to make it a favorite sport.

WOODCOCK FIRE-HUNTING.

"'Tis murderous, but profitable."—*Tom Owen.*

ONE of the most beautiful and " legitimate " amusements
of gentlemen, is woodcock shooting. In the " back-
woods," where game of every kind is plentiful, it is pursued as often as a necessary of life, as for the gratification afforded by the sport.

Persons living in the hotbeds of civilization, but
who yet retain enough of the old leaven of the wild man,
to love to destroy the birds of the air, and the beasts of
the field, are obliged to eke out the excitements of the
field by conventional rules, which prescribe the manner
of killing, the weapon to be used, and the kind of dog
to be employed ;—and the sportsman who is most correct
in all these named particulars, is deservedly a " celeb-
rity " in his day and generation.

No sport is more properly guarded and understood
by amateur hunters than woodcock shooting, and no
sport is more esteemed. Therefore, it was that the announcement that there was a section of the United

10*

States where the game bird was hunted by torchlight, and killed " without the benefit of clergy," created the same sensation among the " legitimists," as is felt at Saint Germain's, because there is " no Bourbon on the throne " —a thrill of horror pervaded the hearts of many who could believe such a thing *possible*—while the more " strait laced " and deeply conscientious, disbelieved entirely, and pronounced the report too incredible for any thing but a " hoax." Yet, woodcock fire-hunting is a fact, although most circumscribed in its geographical limits, the reasons for which, will appear in the attempt at a description of the sport.

Woodcock fire-hunting is almost entirely confined to a narrow strip of country running from the mouth of the Mississippi, up the river about three hundred miles. This narrow strip of country is the rich and thickly settled land that borders on the river, and which varies from one to three miles in width ; it is in fact nothing but the ridge or high ground that separates the Mississippi from the interminable swamps, that compose so great a portion of the State of Louisiana.

The habits of the woodcock make it entirely a nocturnal bird ; it retires into these swamps that border its feeding grounds during the day, and is perfectly safe from interruption ; hidden among the tangled vines, cane-brakes, and boggy land, it consults alike its pleasure and safety ; finds convenient places for its nests, and raises its young, with the assurance of being undisturbed. As a matter of course they increase rapidly, until these solitudes become alive with their simple murmuring note ; and when evening sets in, they fill the high land which we have described, in numbers which can scarcely be imagined by any one except an eye-witness.

Another cause, probably, of their being so numerous in this section of the country may be owing to their migratory habits, as the bird is seen as far north as the river St. Lawrence in summer, and we presume that these very birds return for their winter residence in Louisiana in the very months when "fire-hunting" is practised, which is in the latter part of December, January, and the first part of February.

Yet, a resident in the vicinity or among the haunts of these birds, may live a life through, and make day hunting a business, yet be unconscious that woodcock inhabit his path ; so much is this the case, that I do not know of the birds ever being hunted, in the common and universal way, in the places where fire-hunting them is practised.

This novel sport, we presume, originated among the descendants of the French, who originally settled on the whole tract of country bordering on the Mississippi, as high up as it favors this kind of sport. Here it is, that "Beccasse" forms a common dish when in season, in which the poor and the wealthy indulge as a luxury, too common to be a variety, and too excellent not to be always welcome.

With these preliminaries let us prepare for the sport.

Provide yourself with a short double-barrelled fowling-piece of small bore; let your ammunition be first-rate, and have something the size of a small thimble wherewith to measure out your load of mustard shot. Let your powder be in a small flask, but keep your shot loose with your measure, in the right side pocket of your shooting jacket—and, astonished sportsman! leave thy noble brace of dogs shut up in their kennels; for we would hunt woodcock, incredible as it may seem, without them.

In the place of the dogs we will put a stout negro, who understands his business, burdened with what resembles an old-fashioned warming-pan, but the bottom, instead of the top, pierced with holes; in this pan are small splinters of pine knot, and we denominate this, the Torch. Then put on the broad-brimmed palmetto hat, so that it will shade your eyes, and keep them from alarming the birds. Now, follow me down into any of the old fields that lie between the river and the swamp, while the ladies can stand upon spacious galleries that surround the house, and tell by the quick report of guns our success; the streaming light from " the torch," will, to them, from the distance, look like an ignis fatuus dancing the cachuca in the old field.

It is in the middle of January, the night is a favorable one, the weather rather warm, the thermometer says

" temperate," and the fog rolls off the cold water into the river like steam ; an old " fire-hunter " says, " this is just the night."

Whiz—whiz—hallo ! What's here ? Sambo strike a light, and hoist it over your head. Now, friend, place yourself behind the torch, on the left, both of us in the rear to court the shade. Now, torch-bearer, lead on. Whiz—bang—whiz, bang—two woodcock in a minute. Bang, bang. Heavens, this is murder ! Don't load too heavy—let your charges be mere squibs, and murder away,—the sport is fairly up.

The birds show plainly from three to ten paces all around you, and you can generally catch them on the ground, but as they rise slowly and perpendicularly from the glare of the light, with a flickering motion, you can bring them down before they start off like arrows into the surrounding darkness. Thank the stars they do not fly many paces before they again alight, so that you can follow the same bird or birds until every one is destroyed. Bang, bang—how exciting—don't the birds look beautiful as they stream up into the light ; the slight reddish tinge of their head and breast shining for an instant in the glare of the torch like fire.

Ha! see that stream of gold, bang—and we have a meadow-lark, the bright yellow of its breast being more beautiful than the dull colors of the woodcock. And I see, friend, you have bagged a quail or two. Well, such things occasionally happen. Two hours sport, and we have killed between us nearly thirty birds. With old hunters the average is always more, and a whole night's labor, if successful, is often rewarded with a round hundred.

Practice and experience, as a matter of course, have much to do with success in this sport, but less than in any other; for we have known tyros, on one or two occasions, to do very well with clubs; while the negroes have thrashed them down by "baskets-full" with whips made of bundles of young cane, the birds being so thick that some could be brought down even in this way, while endeavoring, in their confusion, to get out of the glare of the torch.

This fact, and the quantity of birds killed, attest to the extraordinary numbers that inhabit this particular section of country.

Let the birds, however, be less numerous than we have described, and they are on some days more plentiful than on others, and one who is a good shot, in the ordinary way of hunting the bird, has only to overcome his astonishment, and we will add, horror, at the mode in which he sees his favorite game killed, to be a perfect master of woodcock fire-hunting under all circumstances. It is common with those who are fond of sport, and have some sentiment about them, never to fire until the bird rises, and then to bring down a bird with each barrel.

This requires quick shooting, as the torch only sheds

an available light in a circle of about twenty yards in diameter. Parties are frequently made up who hunt during a given number of hours, and the destruction of the birds on these occasions is almost beyond belief.

These parties afford rare sport, and are often kept up all night.

When this is the case, the sportsman not unfrequently sleeps to so late an hour in the day that he has only time to rise, sip a cup of strong coffee, and leisurely dress for dinner, when it is announced as ready, and woodcock, plentiful to wasting, are smoking on the board before him.

Such a dinner, the dullest intellect can imagine, is a repast both for sense and soul,—for woodcock and wit are synonymous.

WATER CRAFT OF THE BACK-WOODS.

STARTING amid the volcanic precipices, eternal snows, and arid deserts of the Rocky Mountains; the Snake River winds its sinuous way towards the Pacific; at one time, rushing headlong through the deep gorges of the mountains, and at another, spreading itself out in still lakes, as it sluggishly advances through ever-varying scenes of picturesque grandeur and of voluptuous softness.

In all this variety, the picture only changes from the beautiful to the sublime; while the eye of the civilized intruder, as it speculates on the future, can see on the Snake River, the city, the village, and the castle, in situations more interesting and more romantic than they have ever yet presented themselves to the world.

The solitary trapper and the wild Indian are now the sole inhabitants of its beautiful shores; the wigwams of the aborigine, the temporary lodge of the hunter and the cunning beaver, rear themselves almost side by side, and nature reposes like a virgin bride in all her beauty and loveliness, soon to be stripped of her natural charms to fulfil new offices with a new existence.

On an abrupt bank of this beautiful stream, overlooking the surrounding landscape for miles—a spot of all others to be selected for a site of beauty and defence, might be seen a few lodges of the Wallawallah Indians.

On the opposite shore stood a fine young warrior, decked in all the tinsel gewgaws which his savage fancy had suggested, to catch the love of his mistress. With stealthy steps he opened the confused undergrowth that lined the banks, and taking therefrom a delicate paddle, he fruitlessly searched until the truth flashed upon him, that some rival had stolen his canoe. Readily would he have dashed into the bosom of the swollen river, and, as another Leander, sought another Hero, but his dress was not to be thus spoiled. Like a chafed lion he walked along the shore, his bosom alternately torn by rage, love, and vanity, when, far up the bank he saw a herd of buffalo slaking their thirst in the running stream. Seizing his bow and arrow, with noiseless step he stole upon his victim, and the unerring shaft soon brought it to the earth, struggling with the agonies of death.

It was the work of only an adept to strip off the skin and spread it on the ground. Upon it were soon laid the gayly wrought moccasons, leggings, and hunting shirt—the trophies of honorable warfare, and the skins of birds of beautiful plumage. The corners of the hide were then brought together, and tied with thongs; the bundle was set afloat upon the stream, and its owner dashed on the rear, guiding it to the opposite shore with its contents unharmed.

Again decking himself, and bearing his wooing tokens before him, he ran with the swiftness of the deer to the lodge that contained his mistress, leaving the *simplest of all the water-craft* of the back-woods to decay upon the ground.

The helplessness of age, the appealing eyes and hands of infancy, the gallantry of the lover, the hostile excursion of a tribe, are natural incentives to the savage mind to improve upon the mere bundle of inanimate things that could be safely floated upon the water. To enlarge this bundle, to build up its sides, would be his study and delight, and we have accordingly next in the list of back-woods craft, what is styled by the white man, —the *Buffalo-skin boat*. This craft is particularly the one of the prairie country, where the materials for its construction are always to be found, and where its builders are always expert.

A party of Indians find themselves upon the banks of some swift and deep river—there is no timber larger than a common walking stick to be seen for miles around; the Indians are loaded with plunder—for they have made a successful incursion into the territory of some neighboring tribe, and cannot trust their effects in the water; or they are perchance migrating to a favorite hunting ground, and have with them all their domestic utensils, their squaws and children. A boat is positively necessary, and it must be made of the materials at hand. A fire is kindled, and by it are laid a number of long slender poles, formed by trimming off the limbs of the saplings growing on the margin of the stream. While this is going on, some of the braves start in pursuit of buffalo; two of the stoutest bulls met with, are killed and stripped of their skins. These skins are then sewed together, the poles having been well heated, the longest is selected and bent into the proper form for a keel; the ribs are then formed and lashed transversely to it, making what would appear to be the skeleton of a large animal. This skeleton is then placed upon the hairy side of the buffalo skin, when it is drawn around the frame and secured by holes cut in the skin, and hitched on to the ribs; a little pounded slippery-elm bark is used to caulk the seams, and small pieces of wood cut with a thread-like screw, are inserted in the arrow or bullet holes of the hide.

Thus, in the course of two or three hours, a handsome and durable boat is completed, capable of carrying eight or ten men with comfort and safety.

Passing from the prairie we come to the thick forest, and there we find the most perfect of the water-craft of the back-woods—the varieties of the canoe. The in-

habitant of the woods never dreams of a boat made of
skins; he looks to the timber for a conveyance. Skilled
in the knowledge of plants, he knows the exact time
when the bark of the tree will most readily unwarp from
its native trunk; and from this simple material he forms
the most beautiful craft that sits upon the water.

The rival clubs that sport their yachts upon the
Thames, or ply them upon the harbor of Mannahatta,
like things of life—formed as their boats are by the high
scientific knowledge and perfect manual skill of the two
great naval nations in the world, are thrown in the
shade by the beautiful and simple bark canoe, made by
the rude hatchet and knife of the red man.

The American forest is filled with trees, whose bark
can be appropriated to the making of canoes; the pecan,
and all the hickories, with the birch, grow there in infinite
profusion.

A tree of one of these species that presents a trunk
clear of limbs for fifteen or twenty feet, is first selected;
the artisan has nothing but a rude hunting knife and
tomahawk for the instruments of his craft; with the latter, he girdles the bark near the root of the tree—this
done, he ascends to the proper height, and there makes
another girdle; then taking his knife and cutting
through the bark downwards, he separates it entirely
from the trunk.

Ascending the tree again, he inserts his knife-blade
under the bark, and turning it up, soon forces it with

his hand until he can use more powerful levers; once well started, he will worm his body between the bark and the trunk, and thus tear it off, throwing it upon the ground, like an immense scroll. The *ross*, or outside of the bark, is scraped off until it is quite smooth, the scroll is then opened, and the braces inserted in order to give the proper width to the gunnels of the canoe. Strong cords are then made from the bark of the linn tree or hickory, the open ends of the bark scroll are pressed together and fastened between clamps, the clamps secured by the cord. If the canoe be intended only for a temporary use, the clamps are left on.

But if to usefulness there can be added the highest beauty, then the rude clamps are displaced by the sewing together of the ends of the bark. A preparation is then made of deer's tallow and pounded charcoal, which is used instead of pitch to fill up the meshes of the seams, and the boat is complete.

This simple process produces the most beautiful model of a boat that can be imagined; art can neither embellish the form, or improve upon the simple mechanism of the back-woods. Every line in it is graceful, and its sharp bows indeed seem almost designed to cleave the air as well as water, so perfectly does it embrace every scientific requisite for overcoming the obstructions of the element in which it is destined to move. In these apparently frail machines, the red man, aided but by a single paddle, will thread the quiet brook and deep running river, speed over the glassy lake like a swan, and shoot through the foaming rapids as sportively as the trout, and when the storm rages, and throws the waves heavenward, and the lurid clouds seem filled with molten fire, you will see the Indian, like a spirit of the storm, at one time standing out in bold relief against the lightning-riven sky, the next moment—disappearing in the watery gulf, rivalling the gull in the gracefulness of his movements, and rejoicing, like the petrel, in the confusion of the elements.

The articles used in savage life, like all the works of nature, are simple, and yet perfectly adapted to the purpose for which they are designed.

The most ingenious and laborious workman, aided by the most perfect taste, cannot possibly form a vessel so general in its use, so excellent in its ends, as the calabash.

The Indian finds it suspended in profusion in every glade of his forest home, spontaneous in its growth, and more effectually protected from destruction from animals, through a bitter taste, than by any artificial barrier whatever. So with all the rest of his appropriations from nature's hands. His mind scarcely ever makes an effort, and consequently seldom improves.

The simple buffalo skin that forms a protection for the trifles of an Indian lover, when he would bear them safely across the swollen stream, compared with the gorgeous barge that conveyed Egypt's queen down the

Nile to meet Antony, seems immeasurably inferior in skill and contrivance. Yet the galley of Cleopatra, with all its gay trappings, and its silken sails glittering in the sun, was as far inferior to a "ship of the line," as the Indian's rude bundle to the barge of Cleopatra.

Imagination may go back to some early period, when the naked Phœnician sported upon a floating log ; may mark his progress, as the inviting waters of the Mediterranean prompted him to more adventurous journeyings, and in time see him astonishing his little world, by fearlessly navigating about the bays, and coasting along the whole length of his native home.

How many ages after this, was it, that the invading fleets of classic Greece, proud fleets, indeed, in which the gods themselves were interested, were pulled ashore, as now the fisherman secures his little skiff? Admire the proud battle ship, riding upon the waves, forming a safe home for thousands, now touching the clouds with its sky-reaching masts, and descending safely into the deep. With what power and majesty does it dash the intruding wave from its prow, and rush on in the very teeth of the winds !

Admire it as the wonder of human skill, then go back through the long cycle of years, and see how many centuries have elapsed in thus perfecting it—then examine the most elaborate craft of our savage life, and the antiquity of their youth will be impressed upon

PLACE DE LA CROIX.

A ROMANCE OF THE WEST.

THERE is much of beautiful romance in the whole history of the early settlements of Florida. De Soto and Ponce de Leon have thrown around the records of their searches for gold and the waters of life, a kind of dreamy character which renders them more like traditions of a spiritual than of a real world. They and their followers were men of stern military discipline, who had won honors in their conquests over the Moors; and they came hither not as emigrants, seeking an asylum from oppression, but as proud nobles, anxious to add to their numerous laurels, by conquests in a new world. The startling discoveries,—the fruits, the gold, and the natives that appeared with Columbus at the court of Isabella,—gave to fancy an impetus, and to enthusiasm a power, which called forth the pomp of the "Infallible

Church " to mingle her sacred symbols with those of arms ; and they went joined together through the wilds of America.

Among the beautiful and striking customs of those days, was the erection of the Cross at the mouths of rivers, and prominent points of land, that presented themselves to the discoverers.

The sacred symbol thus reared in solitude, seemed to shadow forth the future, when the dense forests would be filled with its followers, instead of the wild savage ; and it cheered the lonely pilgrim in his dangerous journeys, bringing to his mind all the cherished associations of this life, and directing his thoughts to another world. In the putting up of these crosses, as they bore the arms of the sovereign whose subjects erected them, and as they were indicative of civil jurisdiction and empire, the most prominent and majestic locations were selected, where they could be seen for miles around, towering above every other object, speaking the advances of the European, and giving title to the lands over which they cast their shadows.

Three hundred years ago the sign of the cross was first raised on the banks of the Mississippi.

From one of the few bluffs or high points of land that border that swift-running river, De Soto, guided by the aborigines of the country, was the first European that looked upon its turbid waters, soon to be his grave. On this high bluff, taking advantage of a lofty cotton-

11

wood tree, he caused its majestic trunk to be shorn of its limbs; and on this tall shaft placed the beam which formed the cross.

This completed, the emblazoned banners of Spain and Arragon were unfurled to the breeze, and, amid the strains of martial music and the firing of cannon, the steel-clad De Soto, assisted by the priests in his train, raised the host to heaven, and declared the reign of Christianity commenced in the valley of the Mississippi.

The erection of this touching symbol in the great temple of nature was full of poetry. The forests, like the stars, declare the wonderful works of the Creator. In the silent grandeur of our primeval woods, in their avenues of columns, their canopies of leaves, their festoons of vines, the cross touched the heart, and spoke more fully its office than ever it will glistening among the human greatness of a Milan cathedral, or the solemn grandeur of a St. Peter's.

Two hundred years after Ponce de Leon had mingled his dust with the sands of the peninsula of Florida, and De Soto reposed beneath the current of the Mississippi, the same spirit of religious and military enthusiasm pervaded the settlements made by both French and Spanish in this " land of flowers."

Among the adventurers of that day were many who mingled the romantic ambition of the crusaders with the ascetic spirit of the monk, and who looked upon themselves as ambassadors of religion to new nations in a new world. Of such was Rousseau. It requires little imagination to understand the disappointment that such a man would meet with in the forest, and as an intruder of the untractable red man. The exalted notions of Rousseau ended in despondence, when away from the pomp and influence of his church. Having been nurtured in the " Eternal City," he had not the zeal, and lacked the principle, to become an humble teacher to humbler recipients of knowledge.

Disregarding his priestly office, he finally mingled in the dissipations of society, and in the year 1736, started off as a military companion to D'Arteguette in his expedition among the Chickasas.

The death of D'Arteguette and his bravest troops, and the dispersion of his Indian allies, left Rousseau a wanderer, surrounded by implacable enemies, he being one of the few who escaped the fate of battle.

Unaccustomed to forest life, and more than a thousand miles from the Canadas, he became a prey of imaginary and real dangers. Unprovided with arms, his food was of roots or herbs. At night the wild beasts howled round his cold couch, and every stump in the daytime seemed to him to conceal an Indian.

Now it was, that Rousseau reviewed the incidents of his past life with sorrow. He discovered, when it was too late, that he had lost his peace of mind, and his hopes of future existence, for a momentary enjoyment. Wasting with watching and hunger, he prayed to the

Virgin to save him, that he might, by a long life of penance, obliterate his sins. On the twelfth day of his wanderings he sank upon the earth to die, and, casting his eyes upward in prayer, he saw, far in the distance, towering above every other object, the cross!

It seemed a miracle, and inspired with strength his trembling limbs; he pressed forward that he might breathe his last at its foot. As he reached it, a smile of triumph lighted up his wayworn features, and he fell insensible to the earth.

Never, perhaps, was this emblem more beautifully decorated or more touchingly displayed than was the one that towered over Rousseau. From indications, some fifteen years might have elapsed since the European pilgrim had erected it. One of the largest forest trees had been chosen that stood upon the surrounding bluffs; the tall trunk tapered upward with the proportion of a Corinthian column, which, with the piece forming the cross, was covered with ten thousand of those evergreen vines that spread such a charm over the southern landscape. It seemed as if nature had paid tribute to the sacred symbol, and festooned it with a perfection and beauty worthy of her abundance. The honey-suckle and the ivy, the scarlet creeper and fragrant jasmine, the foliage enamelled with flowers, shed upon the repentant, and now insensible Rousseau, a shower of fragrance.

Near where he lay, there was a narrow and amply-worn footpath. You could trace it, from where it lost itself in the deep forests, to where it wound around the steep-washed bank, and touched the water's edge. At this point were to be seen the prints of footsteps; and traces of small fires were also visible, one of which, still sent up puffs of smoke.

Here it was that the Choctaw maidens and old women performed their rude labor of washing.

In the morning and evening sun, a long line of the forest children might be seen, with clay jars and skins filled with water, carrying them upon their heads, and stringing up, single file, the steep bank, and losing themselves in the woods;—with their half-clad and erect forms, making a most picturesque display, not unlike the processions figured in the hieroglyphical paintings of Egypt.

Soon after Rousseau fell at the cross, there might have been seen emerging from the woods, and following the path we have described, a delicately-formed Indian girl. In her hand was a long reed and a basket, and she came with blithe steps towards the river. As she passed the cross, the form of Rousseau met her eyes. Stopping and examining him, with almost overpowering curiosity, she retreated with precipitation, but almost instantly returned. She approached nearer, until the wan and insensible face met her view. Strange as was his appearance and color, the chord of humanity was touched, the woman forgot both fear and curiosity, in her anxiety to allay visible suffering. A moment had hardly elapsed before water was thrown in his face and held to his lips.

The refreshing beverage brought him to consciousness. He stared wildly about, and discovered the Indian form bending over him; he again sank insensible to the earth. Like a young doe the girl bounded away, and disappeared.

A half hour might have elapsed, when there issued out of the forest a long train of Indians. At their head was the young maiden, surrounded by armed warriors; in the rear followed women and children. They approached Rousseau, whose recovery was but momentary, and who was now unconscious of what was passing around him. The crowd examined him first with caution, gradually, with familiarity; their whispers became animated conversation, and, finally, blended in one noisy confusion.

There were, among those present, many who had heard of the white man and of his powers, but none had ever seen one before. One Indian, more bold than the rest, stripped the remnant of a cloak from Rousseau's shoulder; another, emboldened by this act, caught rudely hold of his coat, and as he pulled it aside, there fell from his breast a small gilt crucifix, held by a silken cord. Its brilliancy excited the cupidity of all, and many were the eager hands that pressed forward to obtain it. An old chief gained the prize, and fortunately

" He stared wildly about him, and discovered the Indian form bending
over him."—*page* 246.

for Rousseau, his prowess and influence left him in undisputed possession.   As he examined the little trinket, the Indian girl we have spoken of, the only female near Rousseau, crossed her delicate fingers, and pointed upward.   The old chief instantly beheld the similarity between the large and small symbol of Christianity; and extending it aloft, with all the dignity of a cardinal, the crowd shouted as they saw the resemblance, and a change came over them all.

They associated at once the erection of the large cross with Rousseau; and as their shout had again called forth exhibitions of life from his insensible form, they threw his cloak over him, suspended the cross to his neck, brought, in a moment, green boughs, with which a litter was made, and bore him with all respect toward their lodges.   The excitement and exercise of removal did much to restore him to life; a dish of maize did more; and nothing could exceed his astonishment on his recovery, that he should be treated with such kindness; and as he witnessed the respect paid the cross, and was shown by rude gestures, that he owed his life to its influence, he sank upon his knees, overwhelmed with its visible exhibition of power, and satisfied that his prayer for safety had been answered by the accomplishment of a miracle.

The Choctaws, into whose hands the unfortunate Rousseau had fallen (although he was not aware of the difference), were of a kinder nature than the Cherokees, from whom he had so lately escaped.

Years before, the inhabitants of the little village, on their return from a hunting expedition, discovered the cross we have described; its marks then were such as would be exhibited a few days after its erection. Footsteps were seen about its base, which, from their variance with the mark left by the moccasin, satisfied the Indians that it was not erected by any of their people. The huge limbs that had been shorn from the trunk bore fresh marks of terrible cuts, which the stone hatchet could not have made.

As is natural to the Indian mind, on the display of power which they cannot explain, they appropriately, though accidentally, associated the cross with the Great Spirit, and looked upon it with wonder and admiration.

Beside the cross there was found an axe, left by those who had used it. This was an object of the greatest curiosity to its finders. They struck it into the trees, severed huge limbs, and performed other powerful feats with it, and yet fancied that their own rude stone instruments failed to do the same execution, from want of a governing spirit, equal to that which they imagined presided over the axe, and not from difference of material.

The cross and the axe were associated together in the Indians' minds; and the crucifix of Rousseau connected him with both. They treated him, therefore, with all the attention they would bestow upon a being who is master of a superior power.

The terrible and strange incidents that had formed the life of Rousseau, since the defeat of his military associate, D'Arteguette, seemed to him, as he recalled them in his mind, to have occupied an age. His dreams were filled with scenes of torment and death. He would start from his sleep with the idea that an arrow was penetrating his body, or that the bloody knife was at his heart ; these were then changed into visions of starvation, or destruction by wild beasts. Recovering his senses, he would find himself in a comfortable lodge, reposing on a couch of soft skins ; while the simple children of the woods, relieved of their terrors, were waiting to administer to his wants. The change from the extreme of suffering to that of comfort, he could hardly realize.

The cross in the wilderness, the respect they paid to the one upon his breast, were alike inexplicable ; and Rousseau, according to the spirit of his age, felt that a miracle had been wrought in his favor : and on his bended knees he renewed his ecclesiastical vows, and determined to devote his life to enlightening and christianizing the people among whom Providence had placed him.

The Indian girl who first discovered Rousseau, was the only child of a powerful chief. She was still a maiden, and the slavish labor of savage married life had, consequently, not been imposed upon her.

11*

Among her tribe she was universally considered beautiful ; and her hand had been vainly sought by all the young " braves " of her tribe.

Wayward, or indifferent to please, she resolutely refused to occupy any lodge but her father's, however eligible and enviable the settlement might have appeared in the eyes of her associates.

For an Indian girl she was remarkably gentle ; and, as Rousseau gradually recovered his strength, he had, through her leisure, more frequent intercourse with her than with any other of the tribe.   There was also a feeling in his breast that she was, in the hands of an overruling Providence, the instrument used to preserve his life.   Whatever might have been the speculations of the elders of the tribe, as day after day Rousseau courted her society and listened to the sounds of her voice, we do not know ; but his attentions to her were indirectly encouraged, and the Indian girl was almost constantly at his side.

Rousseau's plans were formed.   The painful experience he had encountered, while following the ambition of worldly greatness, had driven him back into the seclusion of the church, with a love only to end with his life.

He determined to learn the dialect of the people in whose lot his life was cast, and form them into a nation of worthy recipients of the " Holy Church ;" and the gentle Indian girl was to him a preceptor, to teach him her language. With this high resolve, he repeated the sounds of her voice, imitated her gesticulations, and encouraged, with marked preference, her society.

The few weeks passed by Rousseau among the Choctaws, had made him one bitter, implacable enemy. Unable to explain his office or his intentions, his preference for Chechoula, had been marked by the keen eye of a jealous and rejected lover.

Wah-a-ola was a young " brave," who had distinguished himself on the hunting and war paths. Young as he was, he had won a name. Three times he had laid the trophies of his prowess at the feet of Chechoula, and as often she had rejected his suit. Astonished at his want of success, he looked upon his mistress as laboring under the influence of some charm, for he could find no accepted rival for her hand.

The presence of Rousseau—the marked preference which Chechoula exhibited for his society, settled, in his own mind, that the " pale face " was the charmer.

With this conviction, he placed himself conveniently to meet his mistress, and once more pleaded his suit before he exhibited the feelings of hatred which he felt towards Rousseau. The lodge of Chechoula's father was, from the dignity of the chief, at the head of the Indian village, and at some little distance. The impatient Wah-a-ola seated himself near its entrance, where, from his concealment, he could watch whoever entered its door. A short time only elapsed, before he saw, in the cold moonlight, a group of Indian girls approaching the Indian lodge, in busy conversation, and conspicuously among them all, Chechoula.

Her companions separated from her, and as she entered her fathers's lodge, a rude buffalo skin shut her in. Soon after her disappearance, the little groups about the Indian village gradually dispersed; the busy hum of conversation ceased; and when profound stillness reigned, a plaintive note of the whip-poor-will was heard; it grew louder and louder, until it appeared as if the lone bird was perched on the top of the lodge that contained Chechoula. It attracted her ear, for she thrust aside the buffalo-skin, and listened with fixed attention. The bird screamed, and appeared to flutter, as if wounded. Chechoula rushed toward the bushes that seemed to conceal so much distress, when Wah-a-ola sprang up and seized her wrist. The affrighted girl stared at her captor for a moment, and then exclaimed,

" The snake should not sing like the birds ! "

Wah-a-ola relaxed not his hold; there was a volcano in his breast, that seemed to overwhelm him as he glared upon Chechoula with blood-shot eyes. Struggling to conceal his emotion, he replied to her question, by asking " If the wild-flowers of the woods were known only to their thorns ? "

" The water-lilies grow upon smooth stones," said Chechoula, striving violently to retreat to her father's lodge.

The love of Wah-a-ola was full of jealousy, and the salute and reply of his mistress converted it into hate. Dashing his hand across his brow, on which the savage workings of his passion were plainly visible, he asked, if "a brave" was to whine for a woman like a bear for its cubs?

"Go!" said he, flinging Chechoula's arm from him: "go! The mistletoe grows not upon young trees, and the pale face shall be a rabbit in the den of the wolf!"

From the time that Rousseau was able to walk, he had made a daily pilgrimage to the cross, and there, upon his bended knees, greeted the morning sun. This habit was known to all the tribe. The morning following the scene between Wah-a-ola and Chechoula, he was found dead at the foot of the sacred tree. A poisoned arrow had been driven almost through his body.

Great was the consternation of the Choctaws. It was considered a mysterious evidence of impending evil; while not a single person could divine who was the murderer.

"The mistletoe grows not upon young trees!" thought Chechoula; and for the first time she knew the full meaning of the words, as she bent over the body of Rousseau. She attended his obsequies with a sorrow less visible, but more deep, than that of her people; although the whole tribe had, in the short residence of the departed, learned to respect him, and to look upon him as a great "Medicine." His grave was dug where he had so often prayed, and the same sod covered him that drank his heart's blood.

According to Indian custom, all that he possessed, as well as those articles appropriated to his use, were buried with him in his grave. His little crucifix reposed upon his breast, and he was remembered as one who had mysteriously come, and as mysteriously passed away.

A few years after the events we have detailed, a Jesuit missionary, who understood the Choctaw language, announced his mission to the tribe, and was by them kindly received. His presence revived the recollections of Rousseau, and the story of his having been among them was told. The priest explained to them his office, and these wild people, in a short time, erected over the remains of Rousseau a rude chapel; his spirit was called upon as their patron saint, and Chechoula was the first to renounce the superstitions of her tribe, and receive the Holy Sacrament of Baptism.

In the year 1829, a small brass cross was picked out of the banks of the Mississippi, near Natchez, at the depth of several feet from the surface. The crucifix was in tolerable preservation, and was exposed by one of those cavings of the soil so peculiar to the Mississippi. The speculations which the finding of this cross called forth, revived the almost forgotten traditions of the story of Rousseau, and of his death and burial at the Place De La Croix.

OPOSSUM HUNTING.

An opossum was made to represent the class of natural *lusus naturæ*, for they are certainly the most singular, inexplicable little animals that live. In their creation, Dame Nature seems to have shown a willingness, if necessary, to be ridiculous, just for the sake of introducing a new fashion. We will not, however, go into particulars, for we might infringe upon the details of "breeding," and thereby "o'erstep the modesty of nature."

One of the peculiarities of the opossum that attracts to it general attention, is the singular pouch they have under the belly, in which their young are carried before their complete development, and also into which they retreat when alarmed by the approach of danger.

This particular organ contains in its interior, ten or twelve teats, to which the young, after what seems a premature birth, are attached, and where they hang for about fifty days, then drop off, and commence a more active state of existence.

This animal evidently varies in size in different lati-
tudes.   In Louisiana they grow quite large compared
with those inhabiting more northern climates.

The opossum ranges in length from twelve to fifteen
inches, the tail is about the same extent.   The body is
covered with a rough coating of white, gray, and brown
hair, so intermixed and rough, that it makes the animal
look as if it had been wet and then drawn through a coal-
hole or ash-heap.   The feet, the ears, and the snout are
naked.

The organs of sense and motion in this little animal
seem to be exceedingly dull.   Their eyes are prominent,
hanging like black beads out of their sockets, and appear to be perfectly destitute of lids, with a pupil simi-
lar to those of a cat, which shows that they are suited
to midnight depredations.

The nostrils of the opossum are evidently well developed, and upon the smell almost exclusively, is it de-
pendent for its preservation.   The ears look as if they
were pieces of dark or soft kid skin, rolled up and fastened in their proper places.   The mouth is exceedingly
large and unmeaning, and ornamented with innumerable
sharp teeth, yet there is very little strength in the jaws.
The paws or hands of the animal are the seat of its
most delicate sensibility, and in their construction are
developed some of the most wonderful displays of the
ingenuity of an All-wise Providence, to overcome the

evident inferiority of the other parts of the animal's construction.

The opossum makes a burrow in the ground, generally found near habitations. In the day time it sleeps, and prowls at night. The moon in its brilliancy seems to dazzle it, for under the bright rays of the queen of night it is often knocked on the head by the negro hunter, without apparently perceiving it has an enemy near.

The habits of the opossum generally resemble those of the " coon " and fox, though they are, as might be supposed from our imperfect description, infinitely less intelligent in defending themselves against the attack of an enemy. Knock an opossum on the head or any part of the body, with a weapon of any kind, small or great, and if he makes any resistance at all, he will endeavor to bite the weapon, instead of the agent using it. The opossum is, in fact, a harmless little creature, and seems to belong to some peace society, the members of which have agreed to act toward the world as the boy promised to do with the bull-dog, " If you will let me alone, I won't trouble you."

Put the animal in a critical situation, and he will resort to stratagem instead of force to elude his pursuers; for if he finds escape impossible, he will feign himself dead in advance of giving you an opportunity to carry out your destructive intentions toward him; or when you think you have destroyed him, he will watch his opportunity, and unexpectedly recovering his breath, will make his escape.

This trick of the little animal has given rise to a proverb of much meaning among those acquainted with his habits, entitled, " playing 'possum," and probably it is as good an illustration of certain deceptive actions of life as can be well imagined.

Take an opossum in good health, corner him up until escape is impossible, then give him a gentle tap on the body that would hardly crush a mosquito, and he will straighten out, and be, according to all indications, perfectly dead. In this situation you may thump him, cut his flesh, and half skin him ; not a muscle will move ; his eyes are glazed and covered with dust, for he has no eyelids to close over them. You may even worry him with a dog, and satisfy yourself that he is really defunct; then leave him quiet a moment, and he will draw a thin film from his eyes, and, if not interfered with, be among the missing.

An Irishman, meeting with one of these little animals in a public road, was thrown into admiration at its appearance, and on being asked why he did not bring the " thing " home with him, said he :

" On sight, I popped him with my shillelah; he died off immadiately, and I thrust the spalpeen into my coat pocket ! ' There's a dinner, ony how,' I said to myself; and scarcely had I made the observation, than he commenced devouring me, biting through my breeches, the

Lord presarve me! I took him out of my pocket, and gave him another tap on the head that would have kilt an Orangeman at Donnybrook Fair: 'Take that for a finis, you desateful crater,' said I, slinging him upon my back. Well, murther, if he didn't have me by the sate of honor in no time. ' Och, ye 'Merica cat, ye, I'll bate the sivin lives out of ye!' and at him I wint till the bones of his body cracked, *and he was clean kilt.* Then catching him by the tail, for fear of accidents, if he didn't turn round and give my thumb a pinch, I'm no Irishman. ' Off wid ye!' I hallooed with a shout, ' for some ill-mannered ghost of the divil, with a rat's tail : and if I throubles the likes of ye again, may I ride backwards at my own funeral!' "

There is one other striking characteristic about the opossum, which, we presume, Shakspeare had a prophetic vision of, when he wrote that celebrated sentence, " Thereby hangs a tail; " for this important appendage, next to its " playing 'possum," is most extraordinary. This tail is long, black, and destitute of hair, and although it will not enable its possessor, like the kangaroo, in the language of the showman, " to jump fifteen feet upwards and forty downwards," still it is of great importance in climbing trees, and supporting the animal when watching for its prey.

By this tail the 'possum suspends itself for hours to a swinging limb of a tree, either for amusement or for the purpose of sleeping, which last he will do while thus "hung up," as soundly as if slipping his hold did not depend upon his own will. This "tail hold" is so firm, that shooting the animal will not cause him to let go, even if you blow his head off; on the contrary, he will remain hung up, until the birds of prey and the elements have scattered his carcass to the winds; and yet the tail will remain an object of unconquered attachment to its last object of circumlocuting embrace.

An old backwoods "Boanerges" of our acquaintance, who occasionally threw down his lap-stone and awl, and went through the country to stir up the people to look after the "consarns of their latter end," enforced the necessity of perseverance in good works, by comparing a true Christian to an opossum up a tall sapling, in a strong wind. Said he, "My brethren, that's your situation exactly; the world, the flesh, and the devil, compose the wind that is trying to blow you off the gospel tree. But don't let go of it; hold on as a 'possum would in a hurricane. If the fore legs of your passions get loose, hold on by your hind legs of conscientiousness; and if they let go, hold on eternally by your tail, which is the promise that the saints shall persevere unto the end."

As an animal of sport, the opossum is of course of an inferior character; the negroes, however, look upon the creature as the most perfect of game, and are much astonished that the fox and deer should be preferred; and the hilarity with which they pursue the sport of 'possum hunting, far excels the enthusiasm of the most inveterate follower after nobler beasts.

Fine moonlight nights are generally chosen on such occasions; three or four negroes, armed with a couple of axes, and accompanied by a cur dog, who understands his business, will sally out for 'possum hunting, and nothing can be more joyous, than their loud laugh and coarse joke on these midnight hunts. The dog scents the animals, for they are numerous, and " barks up the right tree." A torch made of light wood or pitch pine, is soon diffusing a brilliant light, and the axe is struck into the tree containing the game,—let it be a big tree or a small one, it matters not; the growth of a century, or of a few years only, yields to the " forerunner of civilization," and comes to the ground.

While this is going on the dog keeps his eye on the 'possum, barking all the while with the greatest animation. In the mean time, the negroes, as they relieve each other at the work of chopping, make night vocal with laughter and songs, and on such occasions particularly, will you hear " Sitting on a Rail," cavatina fashion, from voices that would command ten thousand a year from any opera manager on the Continent.

The tree begins to totter; the motion is new to the 'possum, and as it descends, the little animal instinctively climbs to the highest limb. Crash, and off he goes to the ground, and not unfrequently into the very jaws of the dog; if this is not the case, a short steeple chase on foot ensues; 'possum finds escape impossible,—feigns himself dead,—falls into the wrong hands, and is at once, really killed.

Such is opossum hunting among the negroes, a sport in which more hard labor is got through with in a few hours than will be performed by the same individuals throughout the whole of the next day. Sometimes two or three opossums are killed,—and if a negro is proud of a yellow vest, a sky-blue stock, and red inexpressibles; with a dead opossum in his possession, he is sublimated.

Among gentlemen, we have seen one occasionally who amuses himself with bringing down an opossum with a rifle, and we have met one who has given the hunt a character, and really reduced it to a science. We were expressing some surprise at the kind manner with which our friend spoke of opossum hunting, and we were disposed to laugh at his taste; we were told very gravely that we were in the presence of a proficient in 'possum hunting, and if we desired, we should have a specimen at sundown, and by the dignity of the hunt we would be compelled to admit that there were a great many ways of doing the same thing. The proposition came from our host, and we at once consented.

The night was *dark*, and I noticed this, and spoke of it; and the reply was, that such a night only, would answer the purpose. A half hour's ride brought us into the depths of the forest, and in the extra darkness of its deep recesses we were piloted by a stout negro bearing a torch. Our dogs—for there were two of them—soon gave notice that we were in the vicinity of an opossum, and finally, directed by their noses—for eyes were of no use—they opened loud and strong, and satisfied us that an opossum was over our heads.

At this moment I was completely puzzled to know how we were to get at the animal, I must confess; we had no axe, and a millstone intervening between the opossum and our eyes, could not have shut it out of sight more effectually than did the surrounding darkness, which seemed to be growing " thicker " every moment, by contrast with the glaring torch.

The negro who accompanied us, without ceremony kindled a large fire about twenty feet from the base of the tree in which our game was lodged, and as soon as it was well kindled and burning merrily, my companion seated himself about forty feet from the base of the tree, bringing the trunk of it directly between himself and the fire. I took a seat by his side by request, and waited patiently to see what would come next. The fire continued to burn each moment more brightly, and the tree that intervened between us and it became more prominent, and its dark outline became more and more distinct, until the most minute branch and leaf was perfectly visible.

" Now," said mine host, " we will have the opossum. Do you see that large knotty-looking substance on that big limb to the right? It looks suspicious; we will speak to it."

The sharp report of the rifle followed, and the negro that accompanied us picked up a large piece of bark that fell rattling to the ground. The rifle was reloaded, and another suspicious-looking protuberance was fired at, and another knot was shattered. Again was the rifle reloaded, and the tree more carefully examined. Hardly had its shrill report awakened the echoes of the forest for the third time, before a grunt that would have done honor to a stuck pig was heard, and the solid fat body of the 'possum fell at our feet. The negro picked it up, relit his torch, and we proceeded homeward.

When reseated by a comfortable fire, we were asked our opinion by our host of "a white man's 'possum hunt;" we expressed our unqualified approbation of the whole affair, although we thought at first that any improvement on the negro's mode of doing the business would be "painting the lily!"

As an article of food the opossum is considered by many a very great luxury; the flesh, it is said, tastes not unlike roast pig. We should have liked very much to have heard "Elia's" description of a dish of it; he found sentiment and poetry in a pig,—where would he have soared to over a dish of 'possum?

In cooking the "varmint," the Indians suspend it on a stick by its tail, and in this position they let it roast before the fire; this mode does not destroy a sort of oiliness, which makes it to a cultivated taste coarse and unpalatable.

The negroes, on the contrary—and, by the way, they are all amateurs in the cooking art—when cooking for themselves, do much better. They bury the body up with sweet potatoes, and as the meat roasts, thus confined, the succulent vegetables draw out all objectionable tastes, and render the opossum "one of the greatest delicacies in the world." At least, so say a crowd of respectable witnesses. We profess to have no experience in the matter, not yet having learned to sing with enthusiasm the common negro melody of

"'Possum fat and 'tater.'"

12

A "HOOSIER" IN SEARCH OF JUSTICE.

ABOUT one hundred and twenty miles from New Orleans reposes, in all rural happiness, one of the pleasantest little towns in the south, that reflects itself in the mysterious waters of the Mississippi.

To the extreme right of the town, looking at it from the river, may be seen a comfortable-looking building, surrounded by China trees; just such a place as sentimental misses dream of when they have indistinct notions of "settling in the world."

This little "burban bandbox," however, is not occupied by the airs of love, nor the airs of the lute, but by a strong limb of the law, a gnarled one too, who knuckles down to business, and digs out of the "uncertainties of his profession" decisions, and reasons, and causes, and effects, nowhere to be met with, except in the science called, par excellence, the "perfection of human reason."

Around the interior walls of this romantic-looking place may be found an extensive library, where all the "statutes," from Moses' time down to the present day, are ranged side by side ; in these musty books the owner revels day and night, digesting "digests," and growing the while sallow, with indigestion.

On the evening-time of a fine summer's day, the sage lawyer might have been seen walled in with books and manuscripts, his eye full of thought, and his bald high forehead sparkling with the rays of the setting sun, as if his genius was making itself visible to the senses ; page after page he searched, musty parchments were scanned, an expression of care and anxiety indented itself on the stern features of his face, and with a sigh of despair he desisted from his labors, uttering aloud his feelings that he feared his case was a hopeless one.

Then he renewed again his mental labor with tenfold vigor, making the very silence, with which he pursued his thoughts, ominous, as if a spirit were in his presence.

The door of the lawyer's office opened, there pressed forward the tall, gaunt figure of a man, a perfect model of physical power and endurance—a western flatboatman. The lawyer heeded not his presence, and started as if from a dream, as the harsh tones of inquiry, grated upon his ear, of,

"Does a 'Squire live here ? "

"They call me so," was the reply, as soon as he had recovered from his astonishment.

"Well, 'Squire," continued the intruder, "I have got a case for you, and I want jestess, if it costs the best load of produce that ever come from In-di-an."

The man of the law asked what was the difficulty.

"It's this, 'Squire: I'm bound for Orleans, and put in here for coffee and other little fixins; a chap with a face whiskered up like a prairie dog, says, says he,

"'Stranger, I see you've got cocks on board of your boat—bring one ashore, and I'll pit one against him that'll lick his legs off in less time than you could gaff him.' Well, 'Squire, *I never take a dar.* Says I, 'Stranger, I'm thar at wunce;' and in twenty minutes the cocks were on the levee, like parfect saints.

"We chucked them together, and my bird, 'Squire, now mind, 'Squire, my bird never struck a lick, not a single blow, but tuck to his heels and run, and by thunders, threw up his feed, actewelly vomited. The stakeholder gave up the money agin me, and now I want jestess; as sure as fogs, my bird was physicked, or he'd stood up to his business like a wild cat."

The lawyer heard the story with patience, but flatly refused to have any thing to do with the matter.

"Prehaps," said the boatman, drawing out a corpulent pocket-book, "prehaps you think I can't pay—here's the money; help yourself—give me jestess, and draw on my purse like an ox team."

To the astonishment of the flatboatman, the lawyer still refused, but unlike many of his profession, gave his would-be client, without charge, some general advice about going on board of his boat, shoving off for New Orleans, and, abandoning the suit altogether.

The flatboatman stared with profound astonishment, and asked the lawyer "If he was a sure enough 'Squire."

Receiving an affirmative reply, he pressed every argument he could use, to have him undertake his case and get him "jestess;" but when he found that his efforts were unavailing, he quietly seated himself for the first time, put his hat aside,—crossed his legs,—then looking up to the ceiling with the expression of great patience, he requested the "'Squire, to read to him the Louisiana laws on cock-fighting."

The lawyer said that he did not know of a single statute in the State upon the subject. The boatman started up as if he had been shot, exclaiming—

"No laws in the State on cock-fighting? No, no, 'Squire, you can't possum me; give us the law."

The refusal again followed; the astonishment of the boatman increased, and throwing himself in a comico-heroic attitude, he waved his long fingers around the sides of the room and asked,

"What all them thar books were about?"

"All about the law."

"Well then, 'Squire, am I to understand that not one of them thar books contain a single law on cock-fighting?"

"You are."

" And, 'Squire, am I to understand that thar ain't no laws in Louisiana on cock-fighting ? "

" You are."

" And am I to understand that you call yourself a 'Squire, and that you don't know any thing about cock-fighting ? "

" You are."

The astonishment of the boatman at this reply for a moment was unbounded, and then suddenly ceased ; the awe with which he looked upon " the 'Squire " also ceased, and resuming his natural awkward and familiar carriage, he took up his hat, and walking to the door, with a broad grin of supreme contempt in his face, he observed,—

" That a 'Squire that did not know the laws of cock-fighting, in his opinion, was distinctly an infernal old chuckel-headed fool ! "

MAJOR GASDEN'S STORY.

No one told a story better than old Major Gasden—
in fact he could detail very commonplace incidents so
dramatically, that he would give them a real interest.
He had met with a little incident on his first visit to
New Orleans, that was to him a source of either constant humor or annoyance. Whichever view he took
of the adventure, gave character to his illustration of it.

The "major," on a certain occasion, formed one of
a happy party, and growing communicative under the influence of genial society and old port, was imprudent
enough to call on several persons near and around him
for songs and sentiments—which calls being promptly
honored,—the Major very unexpectedly found himself
under the immense obligation of doing something for his
friends himself; and as he could not sing, and hated salt
water, he compromised, by relating the following personal adventure.

We give it as nearly verbatim as possible, but must premise, that from an occasional twinkle that we noticed in the Major's eyes, we have never been perfectly satisfied that he did not, to use the language of an Irish friend of ours, "make an intentional mistake."

"There ought to be nothing about a dinner, generally speaking," commenced the Major, "to make it an era in one's history in any way.

"The power merely to gratify the appetite just sufficient to sustain life, is eating in poverty; a life spent merely in gratifying the appetite, is brutal. We like a good dinner, and we sit down to one with that complacency of feeling that denotes a thankfulness, that may properly be called, a silent blessing; yet we feel more pity for a man who recollects his bad dinners, than we do for one who distinctly remembers his good ones. In everyday life, things commemorative often start from the table. 'Do you remember,' says Gustibus, 'that so and so happened the day we ate the fresh salmon?' 'I remember the event,' replies Dulce, 'from that exquisite bon-mot uttered on the occasion.'

"I remember my first dinner in New Orleans as distinctly as I remember my first love. I trust it was impressed upon my mind through the excitement of the intellect, as well as through the gratification of the senses. As I journeyed on to New Orleans for the first time, I naturally suggested to my travelling companion, my desire to be most pleasantly provided for while in the

city, and contrary to his usual custom, he launched forth
in eloquent declamation upon the table of *his* host, drew
pictures of luxuries that threw my most sanguine antici-
pations of good living into the shade, and caused me to
look forward with an interest to the gratification of my
palate that I had never before indulged in.

"I landed on the 'levee' of New Orleans in the middle of the morning; although it was early spring, a glorious sun, such as Pomona loves, was making every thing
look gay; the swollen Mississippi dashed a few waves
over the artificial barrier that confined it to its channel,
and as they crowded along in little rivulets, they spar-
kled like molten silver and gold, indicative, as we thought,
of the wealth which was borne upon its waters, and
paid tribute to the city.

"I need not say where I ate my first dinner in New
Orleans. The dining hall was a long one and the diners
numerous. I made my entrance after the soup dishes
had done their office, and was, of course, a little late.

'It might have been the exercise, or excitement,
or a hastily-eaten breakfast, that made me feel in the
spirit of enjoying a good dinner, for I was unusually
disposed that way; and looked down the long tables,
crowded to excess, with great concern, for fear there
would be no room for me, until that melancholy time,
when gravies cool into water and globules of fat, and
meats are just as warm as when alive; the cruets half
filled, and the cloth awry. I trembled at the prospect,

when, to my inexpressible relief, on my left, near the door, at the top of the two long dining tables, was a small round one, at which sat some six or eight gentlemen. A single chair was unoccupied, and without ceremony, I appropriated it to myself.

" I never saw a man come in late to dinner who did not endeavor to look around on the company present, with that sort of expression which signifies ' Who cares if I did come in late ? ' I looked that way, and happened to feel so too ; and as I cast my eyes on the gentlemen at my right and left, and before me, I paid no attention whatever to the cold stare I met with, as if intending to make me feel that I was intruding.

" In this excellent humor with all the world and myself, I asked the waiter with a loud voice for soup, hot if possible, and I found myself accommodated in the twinkling of a ladle. I went to work lustily to lay the foundation of what my friend in the morning had promised, an *extra splendid dinner*.

" Oysters and fish, as a first course, seem to be founded in nature, reason, and taste,——I accordingly made the reflection to the gentleman on my right—he very formally assented to the proposition, and ate sparingly. I pressed him with great solicitude to follow my example,—and do justice to the viands before him. He suggested that he was troubled with a dyspepsia. This little conversation was received by the whole table with what I remember now, and then for a moment, thought

was an unnecessary quantity of laughter, particularly by
a gentleman at the foot of the table, presuming I sat at
the head.   This person, however, had a sparkling eye
and a rubicund nose, and I concluded that he was easily
pleased, and thought nothing more of the matter; at
the same time feeling great sympathy for my friend on
my right, whom I set down as a very bashful man.

"The venison, all trembling about in its dish, with
its spirit lamps, and wine condiments, was very beautiful
indeed, but to me not so much of a rarity as it would
have been, had I not lived in a country where deer were
plenty.   Determined to call out the bashful man, I observed to him if I had had the arrangement of the
dinner, I should have ordered roast beef, as I had understood New Orleans was growing quite celebrated for
that dish.   The bashful man smiled, the rest of the
table were delighted, and it was agreed that it was a
most valuable suggestion.

"Thus encouraged, I went on to inform all present,
that, the sweetest venison I ever tasted was while
'travelling on the frontier;' that it was not cooked
like the steaks in the chafing dish before us, but merely
jerked off of the carcass, thrown on living coals of fire,
and then while steaming hot, devoured with the simple
addition of pepper and salt.   Hereupon the gentleman
with the rubicund nose, told the bashful man that this
second suggestion of mine was invaluable, and another
unnecessarily hearty laugh followed.

"Prairie hens of a most delicate flavor followed after the meats; they were really delicious; they came from Illinois, somebody said, and showed the enterprise of the landlord of the hotel—so I thought and uttered, and my feelings in this matter were entirely appreciated by the little group around me.

"The *becasse*, as they were announced, excited my unbounded astonishment; there they were, in a large dish, packed side by side 'like newly-married couples,' round as globes, and looking as inviting as ice in August.

"I took one in my plate, turned it over and over, and discovered to my horror that the bird had probably committed suicide by running its own bill through its body, and as I drew it out I ejaculated,

"'Woodcock, as I live!!'"

"My bashful friend responded, 'Exactly so.'

"I helped every body; the birds flew about under my administration as if they were alive and mad, and there was a general display of the most cheering good humor at my beneficent liberality.

"In the mean time, the two long tables of the hotel were deserted, the waiters at them were walking about munching bits of bread and other odd ends, piling up plates, and 'clearing off;' but our little party grew more and more merry and happy, wine, delicious and old, flowed freely; course after course followed, and then came a thousand varieties of the confectioner's skill.

" Toasts and sentiments, really new, were engendered by the old wine, songs sentimental and patriotic ; bosom friends were we all, mingling together as sweetly and harmoniously as the waters of the vale of Avoca.

" For my own part, I was particularly happy in my feelings and remarks, whatever *I said* was received with a roar, in fact I never met with the same number of gentlemen so easily pleased and so congenial.

" The sun gradually sunk in the west, and the suggestion of candles by an attendant proved a signal for departure—one more glass around and a sentiment from myself was to finish. Requesting all to fill to the brim, I raised my glass on high, and thus addressed my friends :

" ' Gentlemen—I have heard much of the fine tables spread in New Orleans, particularly of this hotel, and of the enterprise of its host. I have heard nothing equal to their respective or joint merits (*great applause, the rubicund-nosed man breaking his glass in enthusiasm*). The whole of this affair is only surpassed in my experience, or most inflated dreams, by you, gentlemen (casting a sort of patronising look around me), by you, gentlemen,—in your social, literary, and scientific attainments '—(*tremendous cheering*).

" I concluded, in a halo of glory, with ' A health to our host.'

" This speech or sentiment—was drank to the bottom, two gentlemen fell under the table, and four suspender buttons rattled against the windows opposite me. Shaking hands with all who could go through the ceremony, I left the table, whereon had been eaten the best dinner of my life—where I had met the cleverest party ever assembled to my knowledge; such was my first dinner in New Orleans.

"It was nearly one o'clock at night, when I met my friend with whom I had parted in the morning. I found him in his room suffering from a severe attack of the colic; I was still under the pleasurable excitement of my dinner, its effects were still radiating about my brain like heat from a cooling stove. I was very communicative about the events of the day, and among other things exceedingly grateful to my sick friend for introducing me to such a splendid hotel and to such good dinners.

"'Good dinners,' he groaned, 'do I look as if I had eaten a good dinner? nearly dead from swallowing cabbage and pork.'

"The very mention of such gross aliment made me sick, and I asked him where he dined, with undisguised alarm.

"'In the hotel, to be sure,' was his reply.

"I told him that he was dreaming, and to convince him, gave him a hurried description of my own dinner at the same time and place. The severe pains of the colic could not altogether destroy the mysterious meaning of my friend's eyes as he looked up, and informed me that the table I sat down at was a *private table,* and the dinner that had given me so much satisfaction was a "game dinner," got up at great expense, and under the immediate superintendence of celebrated *bon vivants*.

"The conceit of my ability to amuse a party of strangers at the social board, vanished into thin air; the cause of the wit of my jokes was revealed,—fortunate, indeed, as I was, in eating a good dinner, I was still more fortunate in meeting with a party of gentlemen, who were too delicate to hint at any explanations that would, in their presence, inform me of my amusing mistake.

THE GREAT FOUR-MILE DAY.

[This western sketch was elicited from a celebrated but idle pen, by personal friendship for the " Bee Hunter." Its great merit and originality cannot fail to be widely appreciated.]

THE city of Louisville, in the fall of 1822, was visited by an epidemic, which decimated its population, and converted the dwellings of its inhabitants, erewhile the abodes of pleasantness and hospitality, into houses of mourning. The records of the devastations of the fell intruder, are to be found inscribed upon the headstones that whiten the ancient graveyard of the town, wherein are deposited the bodies of those, who, whilst sojourning upon earth, dispensed the good things of this world with graceful liberality, and made a home for the wayfarer amidst a people upon whom he had no other claim than that of a stranger. The Angel of Death hovered over the devoted city in remorseless ecstasy, pointing the shafts of his exhaustless quiver in every direction, and striking down in preference, the shining objects of public consideration and regard. I was among those who felt the winnowing of his wings as he flitted past my couch in quest of nobler trophies.

All those who were not obliged to remain within the doomed precincts of the city, fled to places afar off; while such as mere necessity required to abide the pestilence, resorted to the most ingenious devices to escape its visitation. Those who were overlooked by the Destroyer in his wrath, were near being starved, as few country people dared bring marketing into the town, and those who did so, only ventured within interdicted limits at certain hours of the day, and right hastily did they retreat to their more salubrious abodes. Amid the general desolation, the incidents of woe were strangely mingled with those that cheated Death, momentarily, of his horrors.

It were a scene that might have provoked the attention of Atropos herself, and made her pause awhile in her terrible vocation, to smile upon the ludicrous means that terror invented to thwart the purposes of Destiny. The emaciated figures of the convalescent citizen, strangely contrasted with the stalwart frame of the hardy yeoman, whilst the cadaverous aspect of the former added to the grotesqueness of the besmeared faces of the latter.

The farmer, moved either by compassion or love of gain to visit the town, as he penetrated the city as far as the market-house, would use amulets and bags of sulphur, and besmeared his nose and lips with tar, to protect him in inhaling the tainted atmosphere; and whilst he exposed his poultry for sale, kept continually burning about his stall aromatic herbs, such as penny-royal, sage and tansy, to appease or appal the dread intent of Azrael.

It was with a bounding heart, that late in September I learned that I was well enough to be removed beyond the sound of the church bell, whose daily tolling announced to me, as I lay prostrate, the death of some schoolmate, whose merry laugh would never more be heard upon the bowling-green; or the demise of some ancient crone or new comer, whose gossip or whose enterprise was the pastime of the youth, or the theme of speculation amongst the fathers of the city. The luxuriant forests had just assumed the russet garb of autumn, as I once more found myself without the city, and right speedily did the bracing country air and association with people whose hearth-stone had not been visited by pestilence, exert their influence in restoring me both to cheerfulness and strength.

My destination was Shelby county, in the neighborhood of the village of that name, where I remained until November. It was during the latter part of October that the events transpired that will form the subject of this brief history, and the character of the incident will probably excuse the digression with which it is begun; for, as will be presently seen, the epidemic had a principal agency in producing the catastrophe, which, had it not happened, would have spared me the task of chronicling an achievement in turf matters, more remarkable than the connection between pestilence and the sequel of these pages.

On the third Saturday (if I remember aright) of October, 1822, the Hon. J—— L—— called for me on his way to the Jockey Club Races, on the four-mile day. He had taken up the impression that a race would be a source of amusement and advantage to me; and in the fulfilment of a humane purpose, had brought along with him an Indian pony, that went by the euphoneous name of "Boots," given as much for shortness, as by reason of the color of the animal, which was an equivocation between a sandy brown and a dingy black —just that of a pair of boots, which had not received the polishing aid of the black for an indefinite period. Astride of this epitome of a horse, I made my first appearance upon a race-course. I was then only ten years of age, and the impressions made upon my mind at that time are more vivid than those of a later day, and of more important character.

There were then no spacious stands erected for the accommodation of visitors. Upon a mound within the circle of the track were collected, what was then considered, a vast number of carriages, containing the aristocratic beauty of the country—though perhaps some of the fair patrons of the turf might at this time, or their daughters for them, turn up their seraphic noses at the rude contrivances that rejoiced at so recent a period in the appellation. About the field were horsemen innumerable, and upon the adjacent hills were thronged the less fortunate spectators, who could muster neither wheeled vehicle, nor four-footed beast for the occasion. The scene was one of animation, and to my young imagination,—of unsurpassable brilliancy.

We had not been long upon the ground before we ascertained that something was amiss. Every body wore an uneasy and fidgetty aspect, the cause of which was soon discovered. By the rules of the Jockey Club, it required *three* entries to make a race. There was no walking over the course, in those days. Every purse taken, had to be won gallantly of at least two competitors. Only two horses had been entered, and the sport seemed about to be broken up for want of a third. There were other nags of " lineage pure " in attendance, but their owners were afraid to start them against the celebrated *Blannerhassett*, and the no less celebrated *Epaminondas*.

In this strait the concourse of assembled people grew ill-natured, and even the ladies pouted in sore disappointment. The owners and trainers of the renowned coursers, which were held apart for want of a go-between, vaunted the performances of their respective nags and looked daggers at the judges, whose *conscientious scruples* would not permit the purse to be taken, but in conformity to the constitution and laws of the club.

The famous racer, J—— H——, hopped about the track with accelerated motion, in calling the public attention to the prominent points of *Blannerhassett*, who was to be abated of his laurels by a rule, which he stigmatized with many epithets, having reference to eternal darkness; whilst Dr. B—— was no less industrious in extolling the merits of *Epaminondas*, who happened to be precisely in the same situation with his competitor.

What was to be done? The ladies were making preparation to leave, and the gentleman had begun to arrange for "scrubbing," when the Judge called out from the stand in a loud voice (trumpets were not then in vogue), "saddle your horses!" What a thrill passed through the crowd! and with what emotions did I hear these sounds.

The public, generally, was greatly overjoyed at the prospect of the race, but, nevertheless, there were many who were anxious to know upon what authority the judges had ordered the horses to be saddled; and these were, generally, the very persons who were most boisterous in abusing them for their obstinacy, when it was apprehended that there would be no sport.

Upon inquiry, it was found out that the Hon. J. L——, in conjunction with three other gentlemen, viz., Hon. J. T——, M. H——, and R. B——, Esqrs., had actually entered a third horse, and thereby made the race, in all respects, conformable to the rules of the club.

The strict constructionists were not satisfied, however, with the announcement of the third entry; they demanded to see the animal—and I well remember the air of ruffled dignity with which the owner of " *Boots* " bade me get up behind him, to have the " great un known " led up to the stand for inspection, and saddled, or rather unsaddled, for the race.

The " *Boots* " party had made the entry with no intention of running him. It was on their part a gratuitous subscription of the sum required, to prevent the spectators from going home in chagrin and disappointment. But when pushed to this extremity, they not only produced the nominee, but actually resolved upon making a brush for the money—as much in derision of the scruples of the malcontents, as in obedience to a certain spirit of the old Adam in them, which revolted against the uncharitable suggestions of collusion bruited about the course, when it was said, that the third entry would not exhibit himself for the contest.

Upon the threshold of his ingress into the theatre of fame, poor " *Boots* " met with an obstacle that well nigh nipped his prospects in the bud. The rules of the club required the pedigree of every horse entered to be stated. Alas, " *Boots* " had neither scutcheon nor ancestry. His age was of little consequence. His present owner had come in possession of him ten years before that time, and consequently he was set down as " aged," a term of scope and verge enough to satisfy the most fastidious. But his pedigree! There was the rub.

" *Boots* " was an orphan upon the paternal side from birth, and the mother's too, so far as any one could say to the contrary. He was what is called *filius nullus*, or nobody's child, and consequently had a right to claim any one for parent he thought fit. His owner plead to be allowed to enter him as " a charity scholar," but this could not be granted. At length a compromise was made, and " *Boots* " appeared upon the field under the following imposing blazon and protection.

"'The Hon. J. L—— enters bl. h. ' *Boots*,' aged; by ' *Tar*,' out of a '*Cuff*' mare, of unknown extraction."

These preliminaries settled, the thorough-breds were saddled, and the saddle was taken off of " *Boots* " for the contest. A negro lad who had ridden him as far as the house where I resided, and who was allowed by his master to go to the races, as he had to wait till they were over to take him home, was mounted upon him. Great was the laughter of the crowd when the horses were about starting. The pawing impatience of the over-trained racers, attracted little attention. The gaze of the multitude was upon the black pony. "*Blannerhassett*" neighed, and "*Epaminondas*" snorted,— but all to no purpose. No one cared to look at them. " *Boots* " was like a Merry Andrew in a deep tragedy—

he had completely upset the gravity of the audience, whose powers of composing themselves to the thoughtful mood becoming the occasion, seemed gone for ever, to the great chagrin of J. H——, and Dr. B——, who cavorted about in their anger, as much as their horses.

FIRST HEAT.—There was great difficulty in starting the horses. Several false "get offs" were made. The *star* actors in the drama pirouetted most provokingly, whilst the rider of "*Boots*" made *him* toe the line, where he waited with meekness and humility for the word "go," and even after *that* was given, manifested little anxiety to change his position.

The thorough-breds went at it, pell-mell. The undue share of attention given to "*Boots*" by the crowd, had first nettled their owners and afterwards their jockeys. Away they went like twin bullets, leaving "*Boots*" so far behind, that before the first mile was done he was lost sight of. When they entered the quarter stretch of the close of the second mile, "*Boots*" was for the first time passing the judges' stand. On they went with resistless fury.

In the beginning of the third mile "*Boots*," was seen about a hundred yards in advance. This somewhat startled the spectators, who in the closeness of the running between "*Blannerhassett*" and "*Epaminondas*" had for a moment forgotten all about him. There he was though, in front, and pegging away with hearty good will—ahead it is true in point of position, but actually a mile behind. In a moment they were upon him.

" *Boots* " strove for about six feet to keep his position in advance, but they swept by him, and after they had gone out of sight the good old horse had all his running to himself, and cut out the work to his own liking.

The fourth mile of the race was run under whip and spur; first " *Blan* " and then " *Pam* " (as the spectators abreviated their learned names) was ahead; the feeling of the multitude was intense. In entering the quarter stretch the last mile " *Boots* " was once more discernible, and nothing daunted by the clatter of hoofs, or dispirited by the gibes of such as happened to catch a glimpse of him, was maintaining his accustomed gait steadily, and just rounded the turn, as the "two bloods" swept by the stand—*a dead lock.*

According to the rules of the club, a dead heat was regarded as though none had been run. The Boots party contended that their horse was not distanced, and to this view of the case, the judges unanimously inclined. Upon examination, the rules were positive upon the subject, and had " *Boots* " bolted, or had he not run a foot much less *two miles* of the four, he would be entitled to start a second time. Indeed, no objection was made by any one, none could be made, and accordingly it was determined to put him again in the field—the fact of the matter being, that his owner perceiving that the old

13

horse looked better for his exertion, was inclined to see the day out, just for the fun of the thing.

If the extra exercise of the race improved "*Boots*," it had quite a contrary effect upon the others. They were sadly blown, and manifested growing symptoms of distress. In those days, the business of training a horse for a four-mile race was beyond the skill of Western jockeys, or at least of many of them, and the art of riding in a manner to keep a horse together, and husband him for after heats, was known to but few. In the present case, the horses were both over-trained, and over-worked in the race.

As soon as the heat was done, innumerable boys and grown-up men were rubbing them down, scraping the foam off of them with great industry and perseverance. Covers of brightest colors were put over them, and such pains as few invalids get, were bestowed upon them; whilst his rider hitched "*Boots*" to a post, and quietly sauntered off to a booth, to comfort himself with ginger-bread and a glass of cider.

When the time allowed for rest had elapsed, the three horses were again brought to the post—but this time the thorough-breds had become quite subdued, either through fatigue, or from an admiration of the sober deportment of the strange competitor who stood beside them. At the word "go," they all three "got off" cleverly together for the

Second Heat.—"*Boots*" took a position close up,

which, by the help of such coaxing as was inherent in a stout cane used by *Jesse* (the black boy who rode him), he maintained with wonderful precision. The *cracks* went off at a slow gallop; both riders being ordered to go gently along. In this way they ran the first mile. The second mile was done in the same manner, and now for the first time was heard the exhortation, "go it, *Boots*," as the little black kept closely up. The pace did not improve the third mile, both Dr. B—— and J. H—— knowing that neither horse had more than a short brush in him. Upon the fourth mile the speed did not quicken, until Jesse, taking heart from his closeness to the leading horses, actually challenged the hindermost one for the front. Such a shout as went up upon this rally, was never before heard upon that field.

"Go it, *Boots*," burst from every mouth, and even the ladies moved their 'kerchiefs and murmured soft applause. But chivalrous as the effort was, it came near costing "*Boots*" the laurels that were wreathing for his brow. The push was made too soon. The jockeys became cognizant of the proximity of the unheralded scrub, and went off at the top of the speed of their respective horses. "*Boots*" was fast falling into the rear; but as good luck would have it, they could not quite distance him, but in attempting to do so, they completely used up the "*cracks*."

Epaminondas won this heat by a neck. The stable boys again got around the descendants of Godolphin,

who indeed required their attention more than ever
—-for though they had not run more than half a mile of
the heat, that was enough to worst them terribly in their
jaded condition. And " *Boots*," too, fared better than
before. He was getting to be a feature in the race, and
a circumstance attending the betting made him now an
object of the greatest interest.

After the dead heat, the betting began. The result
of that heat proved the horses to be so nearly of equal
speed and spirit, that great confidence was placed in the
representations of their owners, and parties betted as
they were partial to the one or the other of them

It so happened that no one seemed to take " *Boots* "
into the account in making bets, and by that very means
he had as much money depending upon him as either of
the other horses.

Every one who proposed a wager, betted that either
Dr. B——'s " Pam " or J. H——'s " Blan " would win
the purse.

Now the takers of such offers were ot course " fielders;" for they in fact betted, that the horse named would
not take their money, and consequently, if " *Boots* " won
it, they were as much gainers as though the nag they
relied upon had won it. Hence every bet taken was, in
technical term, upon " the field," though the party that
took it, might have forgotten at the time that there was
such a horse as " *Boots*."

It will be seen that a tissue of accidents first brought

the little *black* upon the field, enabled him to start for the second heat, procured for him a vast number of unconscious backers, and made him, at the present stage of the race, quite a topic of speculation.

As a matter of course, his comfort came to be provided for; and one assiduous groom ventured to scrape him down with a thin lath. Whereupon " *Boots*," who had never been known to perspire since the last war, when he was taken in Canada by the person of whom his present owner purchased him; looked around, and not being able to recognize the fellow, or divine what on earth he was up to, kicked out his left hind leg in evident disgust.

This was the only token of concern in the proceedings going on, that the pony had given during the day, but that, slight as it was, gave great hope to the " fielders," for the other horses, albeit so spry in the beginning, had got beyond the kicking point; and submitted to the manipulation of their trainers with commendable, but ominous docility.

When the interval of rest between the heats had expired, " *Boots* " alone, seemed qualified for a repetition of the preceding exercises. He first made his appearance at the post, in consequence of his not requiring time for saddling. He stood for some moments quietly, as usual, with his nose on a parallel with the judges' stand; but as the trainers brought up *Epaminondas* and *Blannerhassett* he turned his head sidewise, looked wistfully for a moment upon them, and exhaled a long, deep sigh—whether of pity at the dejected aspect and distressed condition of the whilom gallant steeds, or on account of some faint notion of the business he was engaged in, then for the first time penetrating the integuments of his simple understanding, has not been satisfactorily explained.

Had he been aware that money was staked upon him,—that he was in fact accessory to gambling,—it is a question if he would not have sulked outright; for "Boots," although bred in a savage country, had kept moral society for many years; and must have imbibed serious, and temperance ideas. But the word "go" was given, and they were all three off for the

THIRD HEAT.—For the first time the little black was ahead, both in point of fact and position. He went off just as at the commencement of the race, with perhaps a trifle more alacrity from practice.

Jesse, who had been lectured upon the impropriety of his brush in the second heat, so soon as the last half of the fourth mile, imagined that he had done wrong in taking the lead, and set about holding the pony up until the others passed by; but "Boots," to the sore mortification of his rider, would not be held up. He had got a taste of the boy's bludgeon, and not liking its savor, pushed on, despite the most obstinate endeavors to restrain his impetuosity.

The thorough-breds this time, not only could endure

the black's proximity, but absolutely trailed him the whole of the first mile. On entering the second, either through mortified pride, or more positive malice, both the jockeys were ordered to go ahead of the *scrub*. Spurs were put in requisition, and the flagged and worn horses got by the pony before they came into the back stretch. After shaking off their ignoble competitor, they relapsed into the stinted stride they set out with. But Jesse now had become enamored of the front, and on he urged the pony, who, nothing loth, crawled up to them, and came round the quarter stretch neck and neck with the foremost.

In the straight work, first one and then the other glided by him. But these fits and starts in running could not avail against a steady pace. "*Boots*" *would* come up with them, and at every subsequent attempt it was becoming palpably more difficult to part company with him.

On entering the third mile, *Epaminondas* was evidently lame, and when he tried to widen the distance between him and "*Boots*" on the back stretch, gave up: the little *black* went by him for good, and a shout of applause arose, that had wellnigh made old Entellus's sceptre tremble in his grasp.

The contest was now narrowed down to "*Boots*" and *Blannerhassett*,—and neither of them had won a heat.

The four gentlemen who entered the pony, imme-

diately galloped in every direction over the field, encouraging Jesse to get the descendant of Cuff along;
straight ahead, the little black held the even tenor of
his way, whilst "Blan" would first leave him a rod,
and then drop back to him, in flickering fits of "game
and gravel."

At the beginning of the fourth mile, "*Boots*" was
well up; on going round the turn he passed "Blan" a
neck. (Immense cheering.) In the straight running
"Blan" again sloped by the pony, but remained satisfied with getting ahead the least bit imaginable. This
position was maintained to the turn, when "*Boots*"
came alongside, and before entering the quarter stretch,
drew out a full length in advance, amid deafening shouts
of "go it, Boots," "go it, darkey," "pop him, sooty,"
"give him Jesse;" and such like exclamations of dis-
paraging signification, but used in the most laudatory
sense of approbation.

Jesse, unfortunately, in his eagerness to win the
heat; used his cudgel carelessly, and accidentally gave
the black a clip on the head, which so "disgentled" him
that he turned almost entirely around before he could
be checked. In this way, he lost his advantage just as
he reached the distance stand, and it was well for him
that he had got that far, as "*Boots*" showed the most
implacable resentment to such treatment, and tried to
run in every direction but the right one.

Indeed he had not before exhibited such spirit; he

actually reared up, and wasted enough energy in expos-
tulating against any such phrenological experiments being made upon him, to have won the heat, had it been
properly directed.   He could not be induced to resume
operations until " Blan " had passed the judges' stand,
and was pronounced winner of the heat.

At the termination of this heat, the nature of the
betting was fully developed.   The " Blan " party upon
claiming their stakes—*Epaminondas* being distanced—
discovered that " *Boots* " stood between them and the
spoils.   They had raised a feeble shout upon the issue
of the heat, futile enough; for they assumed to consider
a triumph over " *Boots*" as a sorry affair, but when they
understood that the pony was entitled to start a fourth
time, even that faint ejaculation, melted down to a du-
bious mutter.

The rules of the club required a horse to win one of
the three first heats to enable him to keep upon the
track.   Strange to say there was greater doubt concern-
ing this last mile than there was respecting " *Boots* "
being distanced the first heat.   The judges had great
trouble in deciding the difficulty.   Three heats had been
run, and " *Boots* " had won neither; but then the first
was declared null and void, *ergo*, only two had been, in
law, accomplished.

The Epaminondas party here stepped in, as much
for the principle, as the interest of the thing, and declared that " *Boots* " had a right to run a fourth heat.

13*

Dr. B——, who, now that his horse was distanced, would give his left hand to see J. H——'s nag done the same by, declared openly for the pony; and the judges "being sufficiently advised," decided that way. This was the most reasonable, as well as the most popular judgment; for one half of those who betted on " Blan," being, in sporting terms, "fielders," and who, consequently, could not lose, were vociferous for the continuance of the sport.

This question settled, betters were puzzled how to lay out their money. *Blannerhassett* had yet friends who would not hedge. They could not realize the possibility of his being beat by a scrub like " *Boots*," and J. H—— taking courage from the pony's strange freak at the end of the last heat, vaunted his nag's prowess anew, as well to assure his friends, as to brag off the " *Boots*' " people.

Strange rumors were circulated respecting the condition of each horse. The trainer of " Blan " kept the people, as far as possible, from inspecting the state of his charge, whilst every man, woman and child in the field, that chose to do so, was allowed to look on "*Boots*," and get upon his back too, as to that matter.

The old pony looked none the worse for wear, and how to account for his fantastic behavior, was perplexing enough. Some said he sulked, others that he had given way internally,—one or two insinuated foul dealings. None, however, divined the real cause, except Jesse, who kept it to himself, not even venturing to inform his master that the faithful creature he bestrode had only paused in his career to remonstrate against an unintentional, yet serious and glaring personal injury.

What with the fear of a repetition of the pony's caprices, and the well-founded belief that *Blannerhassett* was used up, the public were in an equipoise in regard to the result. Betting was going on pretty freely, when the horses were summoned to the

LAST HEAT.—The pony showed little change since he last "toed the mark," unless perhaps a dogged air, arising as much from a sense of wrong, as an internal speculation as to whether the affair was ever coming to an end.

Blannerhassett looked worse than his namesake did when charged with high treason. The high-bred steed was in no mood to take on airs. He came up panting and faint, and in his distress took no notice whatever of ' *Boots*," who, as soon as the boy mounted him, manifested a strange anxiety to push on. In his eagerness to get his head out of the way of Jesse's stick, he actually made a false start, and had to be called back.

When the word was given, " *Boots* " got greatly the start. It was enough that Jesse held his cudgel so as to remind him that it was in readiness; away he scampered, regardless alike of the shouts of the multitude, and the abuse of the *Blannerhassetts*, whose horse was quite stiff at the go off, and lost ground considerably for the first half mile. On getting a little warm, he went better, but the pony was in no humor to wait for him.

At the close of the first mile, " *Boots* " was two hundred yards ahead, and pegging away as if the devil was behind him, and a phantom corn heap in front.

Blannerhassett's jockey now used whip and spur to overtake the flying imp—but it was in vain. His horse responded to the steel and lash for a few strides, and then gave out; fatigued,—lamed,—and broken down.

Meanwhile " *Boots*," not having the reputation of *Blannerhassett* before his eyes, but the dread of the cudgel behind him, was rattling it off at a merry pace. Upon entering the third mile of the heat Jesse came in view of his antagonist, pretty near the spot where he was overtaken himself, in the beginning of the day. The boy could not for a time comprehend how " Blan " got before him, and was evidently becoming bewildered with the phenomenon, when the Hon. J. L—— told him to push on, and beat the blooded stock, as far as he had been beaten.

The darkey understanding now that he had gained a mile, showed his ivory to the spectators and his cudgel to " *Boots*," and swept by the done-up nag, like a ball fired out of a cannon charged with slow matches.

I will make no attempt to describe the shouts of the people at the issue, until I can dip my pen in electricity to write in thunder drops,—or in the prism, to depict the eye of beauty as it flashed applause, to the unheralded champion.

This feat achieved,—there was no competitor for

" *Boots* " but the sun. Jesse made it his ambition to finish the race by the light of his rays, and he was as proud as a sceptred monarch, when looking over the heads of the throng that gathered around the victorious " *Boots* " upon the conclusion of the heat, he saw the glorious orb yet above the horizon, and looking gladly upon him as though he would bless him before he went to bed.

" *Boots* " was near sharing the fate of the Grecian, who was smothered to death in the theatre, by wreaths and shawls showered down upon him in glorification. He could scarcely breathe, for the multitudes that pressed upon him in one way or another, to do him honor. And Jesse, too, got a large share of plaudits and dimes conformably; and even I came in for gleanings of regard, as I rode home upon the pony after the jubilation.

There were no cattle-painters there, nor lithographers, nor daguerreotypists; else " *Boots* " and his rider would have been transmitted to posterity in their lineaments of that day. It has fallen upon feeble hands to preserve some faint remembrance of them in this account, which is as inferior to the merits of the theme, as the snuffed candle is to the brilliant orb of day.

THE WAY THAT AMERICANS GO DOWN HILL.

"But who has not been both wearied and amused with the slow caution of the German drivers? At every little descent on the road, that it would almost require a spirit-level to discern that it is a descent, he dismounts, and puts on his drag. On a road of the gentlest undulations, where a heavy English coach would go at the rate of ten English miles an hour, without drag or pause, up hill or down, he is continually alighting and putting on one or both drags, alighting and ascending with a patience and perseverance that amazes you. Nay, in many states, this caution is evinced also by the government, and is forced on the driver, particularly in Bavaria, Wurtemberg, and Austria, by a post by the way-side, standing at the top of every slope on the road, having painted on a board, a black and conspicuous drag, and announcing a fine, of commonly six florins (ten shillings) on any loaded carriage which shall descend without the drag on. In every thing they are continually guarding against those accidents which result from hurry, or slightness of construction."—*Howitt's Moral and Domestic Life in Germany.*

THE stage in which we travelled across "the Alleganics," was one of the then called "Transit line." It was, as the driver termed it, "a rushing affair," and managed, by a refined cruelty to dumb beasts, to keep a little ahead of the "Opposition," which seemed ever to come clattering in our rear, like some ill-timed spirit, never destined exactly to reach, but always to be near us.

The drivers of our different " changes," all seemed to be made upon the go-ahead principle, and looked upon nothing as really disgraceful, but being behind the stage that so perseveringly pursued us.   Unfortunately too, for our safety, we went in an " extra," and managed, by a freak of fortune, to arrive at the different stations, where drivers and horses were changed, just as the former had got comfortably to bed ; and it was not the least interesting portion of my thoughts, that every one of these Jehus made the most solemn protestations, that he would " upset us over some precipice not less than three hundred and sixty-five feet high, and knock us into such a perfect nonentity, that it would save the coroner the trouble of calling a jury to sit upon our remains."

It is nine years since, and if the winter of that year is not set down as " remarkably cold " in the almanacs, it shows a want of care in those useful annuals.

We say it is nine years since we crossed the Alleganies.   At the particular time to which we allude, the " oldest inhabitant " of the country (and we met him on the road side) informed us that he had no recollection of such a severe season.   That we could live through such a night would have been deemed impossible, could its perils have been anticipated, before they were experienced.

The fire in every house we passed smoked like a furnace, and around its genial warmth were crowded groups of men, women, and children, who looked as if they might have been born in the workshop of Vulcan.

The road over which we travelled was macadamized, and then frozen; it was as hard as nature will permit, and the tramping of the horses' feet upon it sounded in the frosty air as if they were rushing across a continuous bridge.

The inside of the stage-coach is a wonder; it is a perfect denial to Newton's theory, that two things, or twenty, cannot occupy the same place at the same time. The one we travelled in was perfectly full of seats, straw, buffalo robes, hat-boxes, rifles, flute cases, and small parcels—and yet nine men—the very nine muses at times (all the cider along the road was frozen, and we drank the heart of it), stowed themselves away within its bowels; but how, we leave to the masters of exhausted air-pumps and hydraulic presses to imagine.

We all, of course, froze, more or less, but it was in streaks; the curtains of the stage were fastened down and made tight, and then, like pigs, we quarrelled ourselves into the snuggest possible position and place; it being considered fortunate to be in the centre, as we then parted with least heat, to satisfy the craving appetite of Jack Frost, who penetrated every little hole and nook, and delighted himself in painting fantastic figures upon the different objects exposed to his influence, out of our misery and breath.

By one of those extraordinary phenomena exhibited

in the climate of our favored country, we unexpectedly found ourselves travelling over a road that was covered with a frozen sleet, for cold as the season was, there was no snow; the horses' shoes consequently had no corks on them worth noticing, and the iron-bound wheels, on this change in the surface of the earth, seemed to have so little hold upon the road that we almost expected they would make an effort to leave it, and break our necks as a reward for their aspirations. On we went, however, and as night came on, the darkness enveloped us in a kind of cloud,—the ice-glazed surface of the ground reflecting upwards a dull, mysterious light.

Our whereabouts never troubled us; all places between the one we were anxious to reach, and where we were, made no impression upon us; and perhaps we would never have known a single particular place, but for the incident about to be detailed.

I think that all my companions, as well as myself, were asleep, when I was awaked by that peculiar sawing motion which a stage body makes upon its springs when suddenly stopped.

"What's the matter now?" was the general exclamation of the "insides" to the driver; who was discovered through the glass window on the ground, beating his arms around his body with a vehemence that almost raised him into the air.

"Matter!" he exclaimed, sticking his nose above a woollen blanket that was tied around his face, which from the cold and his breath was frosted like a wedding-cake, " matter enough ; here we are on the top of Ball Mountain, the drag-chain broken, and I am so confound-edly cold, that I could not tie a knot in a rope if I had eighteen thousand hands."

It was a rueful situation truly.   I jumped out of the stage, and contemplated the prospect near and at a dis-tance, with mixed feelings.   So absorbed did I soon be-come, that I lost sight of the unpleasant situation in which we were placed, and regarded only the appear-ance of things about me, disconnected with my personal happiness.

There stood the stage, upon the very apex of the mountain, the hot steaming breath of my half-smothered travellers pouring out of its open door in puffs like the respirations of a mammoth.   The driver, poor fellow, was limping about, more than half frozen,—growling, swearing, and threatening.   The poor horses looked about twenty years older than when they started, their heads being whitened with the frost.   They stamped with impatience on the hard-ribbed ice, the polished iron of their shoes looking as if it would penetrate their flesh with biting cold.

But such a landscape of beauty—all shrouded in death, we never saw or conceived of, and one like it is seldom presented to the eye.   Down the mountain could be traced the broad road in serpentine windings, lessening in the distance until it appeared no wider than a footpath, obscured by the ravines and forest-trees through which it ran; on each side were deep, yawning chasms, at the bottom of which the hardy pines sprung upward a hundred and fifty feet, and yet they looked from where I stood like creeping plants. The very mountain-tops spread out before me like pyramids. The moon, coming up from behind the distant horizon, shone upon this vast prospect, bathing one elevation of light and another in darkness, or reflecting her silvery rays across the frozen ground in sparkling gems, as if some eastern princess scattered diamonds upon a marble floor; then starting in bold relief the shaggy rock-born hemlock and poison laurel, it penetrated the deep solitudes, and made "darkness visible," where all before had been most deep obscurity.

There too might be seen the heat, driven from the earth in light fogs by the intense cold, floating upwards in fantastic forms, and spreading out in thin ether as it sought more elevated regions.

As far in the distance in every direction as the eye could reach, were the valleys of Penn, all silent in the embrace of winter and night, calling up most vividly the emotions of the beautiful and the sublime.

"How are we to get down this outrageous hill, driver?" bawled out a speculator in the western lands, who had amused us, through the day, with nice calculations of how much he could have saved the government and himself, had he had the contract of making the " National Road " over which we were travelling.

The reply of the driver was exceedingly apt and characteristic.

" There is no difficulty," said he, " in getting down the hill, but you well know there are a variety of ways of doing the same thing; the drag-chain would be of little use, as the wheel-tire would make a runner of it. I think you had better all take your places inside, say your prayers, and let me put off—and if yonder grinning moon has a wish to see a race between a stage and four horses down ' Ball Mountain,' she'll be gratified, and see sights that would make a locomotive blush."

The prospect was rather a doleful one; we had about ninety chances in a hundred that we would make a " smash of it," and we had the same number of chances of being frozen to death if we did not take the risk of being " smashed," for the first tavern we could get to was at the foot of the mountain. The driver was a smart fellow, and had some hostage in the world worth living for, because he was but three days wedded—had he been married six months we would not have trusted him.

The vote was taken; and it was decided to " go ahead."

If I were to describe an unpleasant situation, I should say that it was to be in a stage, the door closed on you, with great probabilities that it will be opened by your head thrusting itself through the oak panels, with the axle of the wheel at the same time falling across your breast. It seemed to me that I would be, with my companions, if I entered that stage, buried alive; so preferring to see the coming catastrophe, I mounted the driver's seat with a degree of resolution that would have enabled me to walk under a falling house without winking.

At the crack of the whip, the horses, impatient of the delay, started with a bound, and ran on a short distance, the boot of the stage pointing to the earth; a sudden reverse of this position, and an inclination of our bodies forward, told too plainly that we were on the descent. Now commenced a race between gravitation and horse flesh, and odds would have been safely bet on the former. At one time we swayed to and fro as if in hammocks; then we would travel a hundred yards sideways, bouncing, crashing about like mad.

A quarter way down the mountain—and the horses with reeking-hot sides and distended nostrils laid themselves down to their work, while the lashing whip cracked and goaded them in the rear, to hasten their speed.

The driver, with a coolness that never forsook him, guided his vehicle, as much as possible, in zig-zag lines across the road. Obstacles, no larger than pebbles, would project the stage into the air as if it had been an Indian-rubber ball, and once as we fell into a rut, we escaped upsetting by a gentle tap from the stump of a cedar tree upon the hub of the wheel, that righted us with the swiftness of lightning.

On we went—the blood starting in my chilled frame diffusing over me a glowing heat, until I wiped huge drops of perspiration from my brow, and breathed in the cold air as if I were smothering. The dull, stunning sound that now marked our progress, was scarcely relieved by the clattering hoofs of the horses, and the motion became perfectly steady, except when a piece of ice would explode from under the wheels as if burst with powder.

Almost with the speed of thought we rushed on, and the critical moment of our safety came. The stumbling of a horse—the breaking of a strap—a too strongly-drawn breath, almost, would have, with the speed we were then making, projected us over the mountain-side as if shot from a cannon, and hurled us on the frozen ground and hard rocks beneath.

The driver, with distended eyes, and with an expression of intellectual excitement, played his part well, and fortune favored us.

As we made the last turn in the road, the stage for an instant vibrated between safety and destruction,— running for several yards upon one side, it displayed two wheels in the air, whirling with a swiftness that rendered them almost invisible. With a severe contusion it righted—the driver shouted—and we were rushing *up an ascent.*

For a moment the stage and horses went on, and it was but for a moment, for the heavy body lately full of life, settled back upon the traces a dead weight, dragging the poor animals in one confused heap downwards, until, shaking violently on its springs, it stood still.

"A pretty severe tug," said one of the insiders to the driver, as he stretched himself, with a yawn.

"Well, I rather think it was," said Jehu, with a smile of ineffable disdain. "I've driv on this road fifteen years, but I never was so near —— as to-night. If I was on t'other side of 'Ball Mountain,' and my wife on this (only three days married, recollect), I would not drive that stage down 'Ball Mountain,' as I have to-night, to keep her from running away with a darkey."

"Why, you don't think there was any real danger, do you?" inquired another 'insider,' thrusting his head into the cold air.

"I calculate I do," said the driver contemptuously. "If the off fore-leader, when I reached the 'devil's rut,'" he continued, "had fallen, as he intended, your body would now be as flat as either back-seat cushion in that stage."

"Lord, bless us, is it possible!" sighed another 'insider;' "but it is all very well we have escaped, and we must run a little risk rather than be delayed in our journey."

Appreciating more than my fellow-travellers, the terrible ordeal through which we had just passed, I have often in my dreams fancied myself on a stage-coach, just tumbling down the ravines that yawn on the sides of " Ball Mountain," and when I have started into wakefulness, I have speculated on that principle of the American character that is ever impelling it forward ; but it never forcibly struck me as a national peculiarity, until I read Howitt's journey down hill among the sturdy Germans of the Old World.

THE END.